EXPERIENCE

BARCELONA

◎ Walking Eye App

YOUR FREE DESTINATION CONTENT AND EBOOK
AVAILABLE THROUGH THE WALKING EYE APP

Your guide now includes a free eBook and destination content for your
chosen destination, all for the same great price as before.
Simply download the Walking Eye App from the App Store or
Google Play to access your free eBook and destination content.

HOW THE WALKING EYE APP WORKS

Through the Walking Eye App, you can purchase a range of eBooks and destination content.
However, when you buy this book, you can download the corresponding eBook and destination
content for free. Just see below in the grey panels where to find your free content and then scan
the QR code at the bottom of this page.

Destinations: Download your corresponding essential destination content from here, featuring recommended sights and attractions, restaurants, hotels and an A–Z of practical information, all for free. Other destinations are available for purchase.

Ships: Interested in ship reviews? Find independent reviews of river and ocean ships in this section, all available for purchase.

eBooks: You can download your free accompanying digital version of this guide here. You will also find a whole range of other eBooks, all available for purchase.

Free access to travel-related blog articles about different destinations, updated on a daily basis.

HOW THE DESTINATION CONTENT WORKS

Each destination includes a short introduction, an A–Z of practical information and recommended points of interest, split into 4 different categories:

• Highlights
• Accommodation
• Eating out
• What to do

You can view the location of every point of interest and save it by adding it to your Favourites. In the 'Around Me' section you can view all the points of interest within 5km.

HOW THE EBOOKS WORK

The eBooks are provided in EPUB file format. Please note that you will need an eBook reader installed on your device to open the file. Many devices come with this as standard, but you may still need to install one manually from Google Play.

The eBook content is identical to the content in the printed guide.

HOW TO DOWNLOAD THE WALKING EYE APP

1. Download the Walking Eye App from the App Store or Google Play.
2. Open the app and select the scanning function from the main menu.
3. Scan the QR code on this page – you will then be asked a security question to verify ownership of the book.
4. Once this has been verified, you will see your eBook and destination content in the purchased ebook and destination sections, where you will be able to download them.

Other destination apps and eBooks are available for purchase separately or are free with the purchase of the Insight Guide book.

CONTENTS

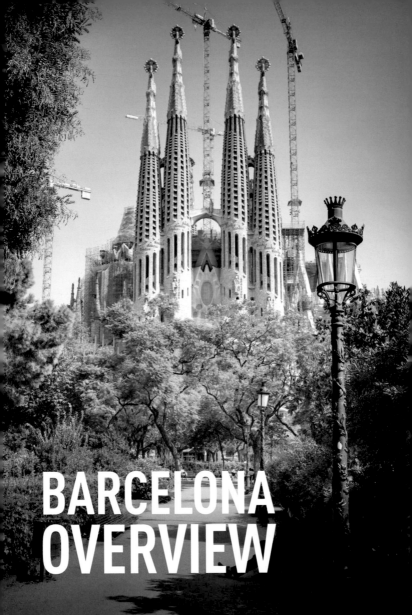

BARCELONA
OVERVIEW

Idyllically nestled between the mountains and the sea, the vibrant, daringly modern city of Barcelona offers everything from Gothic treasures to trendy bars, innovative architecture and exquisite food.

The same things that attracted the Romans to the coastal settlement of Barcino in the 2nd century BC continue to draw people in droves, only now there is the added bonus of Barcelona's contemporary art and design and world-renowned architecture.

The proximity to the sea has brought about cosmopolitanism, a mix of fascinating cultures and an outward-looking people. The Middle Ages' maritime legacy enriched the city with enduring Gothic beauty and a labyrinth of characterful winding lanes in its charming inner barrios. Breaking out of its medieval confines only in the mid-19th century, the sea brought change and exoticism to Barcelona, reflected in its most iconic architecture, Catalan Modernisme. Gaudí and his Catalan art nouveau contemporaries mixed oriental and Moorish influences with sea motifs and curvy wave-like walls.

Radiating out from the waterfront and the Old Town, Ciutat Vella, to the new neighbourhoods developed in the 19th century, the city is dotted with dozens of parks and gardens. Beyond, the chain of hills and mountains form a reassuring protective wall. This is a rare example of an urban and natural paradise rolled into one, where history, phenomenal art and architecture, Catalan culinary traditions, a deep social fibre, edgy contemporary culture and the sea all contribute to a harmonious ensemble. Ildefonso Falcones' 2009 novel *The Cathedral of the Sea* is set in the 14th century against the backdrop of the construction of the Gothic church of Santa Maria del Mar near Barcelona's port, and evokes what a primordial place the sea has in the city. The sea itself is a cathedral of kinds in Barcelona, a mighty and all-pervading presence which moulds everyday life, modern lifestyles, just as it shaped the history of the Catalan capital.

IN THE MOOD FOR...

... HISTORY

Barcelona's ancient history is packed into the Ciutat Vella, the Old Town. Lying within the boundary of the old city wall, it comprises four neighbourhoods: Barri Gòtic, El Raval, Barceloneta, and Sant Pere, Santa Caterina i la Ribera, which in turn includes the trendy El Born district. Here you will find layers of Roman, medieval-Gothic, Renaissance and Baroque history starting with the precious vestiges of the Roman city of **Barcino** (see page 40). The highlight of the Gothic period is the **Catedral de Barcelona** (see page 30), rivalled only by the stained-glass beauties of Santa Maria del Pi and the Ribera's **Santa Maria del Mar** (see page 72). And monarchical history reigns supreme at the **Palau Nacional** (see page 162) and at **Pedralbes monastery** (see page 138), which was founded by a queen.

... VIEWS

Barcelona is awash with lofty views, from the *miradores* of the **Montjuïc gardens** (see page 158) overlooking the port to those in **Park Güell** (see page 143). For less static views hop on the **Montjuïc cable car** (see page 155). There are also dazzling views to behold from the top of several hotels – on Hotel Omm's rooftop they even come with a swim or a yoga class. The Eclipse bar at the **W Barcelona** (see page 93) may be indoors but it does still allow for some bopping and socialising 26 floors high in the sky, and the exclusive 33rd-floor Club rooms and lounge at **Hotel Arts Barcelona** (see page 98) have sweeping views across the marina of Villa Olímpica to the iconic Torre Agbar.

Barcelona has a knack of combining museums with great views, notably at the rooftop cafés and bars of the portside **Museu d'Història de Catalunya** (see page 84), and Montjuïc's **Museu Nacional d'Art de Catalunya** (see page 162) and **CaixaForum** (see page 156). Gaudí was also the master of the most hallucinating sculptured rooftops with views, finding their ultimate expression in the mosaic-splashed patios of the **Casa Batlló** (see page 118) and the **Casa Milà–La Pedrera** (see page 122).

... ART

Barcelona is a city where art and architecture blend in to the most spectacular effect. There is art in everything Gaudí, from his **L'Eixample landmarks** (see pages 118, 122 and 130) to **Park Güell** (see page 143). El Raval is a contemporary art hub boosted by the neighbouring **Museu d'Art Contemporani de Barcelona** (see page 56) and **Centre de Cultura Contemporània de Barcelona** (see page 59), and in L'Eixample cultural institutions such as the **Fundació Antoni Tàpies** (see page 116) are as exquisite outside as they are inside.

For classical art and art history, the place to go is the **Museu Nacional d'Art de Catalunya** (see page 162), the national picture gallery housed within Montjuïc's Palau Nacional. At the other end of the spectrum is **El Born**, Picasso-land (see page 70) but also host to a range of private galleries from the sedate to the more outlandish.

Hit the art gallery trail following sign-posted itineraries promoted by **Art Barcelona** (see page 46), an association of galleries. Various art routes link all major galleries and institutions, with either tangible maps available in hotels or interactive digital maps.

... FAMILY FUN

The wonderland nature of some of Barcelona's most famous architectural landmarks has a strong appeal to children. Gaudí could hardly be described as boring and families can take a dramatised tour of the **Casa Batlló** (see page 118) animated by young Gaudí lookalikes.

At **L'Aquàrium de Barcelona** (see page 81) children aged 8–12 can 'sleep with sharks' while El Poblenou's **Museu Blau** (see page 106) puts on fantastic kid's games and workshops.

Other family-friendly activities include a **Montjuïc cable car ride** (see page 155), a stroll in the **Parc de la Ciutadella** (see page 68) and its **zoo** and of course a **Barça football match** (see page 157). And children of all ages will love the interactive, multimedia **Museu d'Art Contemporani**, Barcelona's Museum of Contemporary Art (see page 56).

... A GOURMET BLOWOUT

With a ready supply of fresh sea-food to dip into, a balmy climate that favours fruit and vegetable production year round, mountain milks and cheeses, olive oils and olives, how could the Catalan cooks possibly go wrong. And all that complemented by Penedès wines and locally made high-shelf vermouths (see page 146).

Hardly surprising then that Barcelona reigns supreme on Spain's Michelin-star scene. Many of the award-winning restaurants are found in swish **L'Eixample** (see page 126), whether you're in the mood for the classics or new Catalan cuisine. The Catalan-born Roca brothers have a big footprint in the city: they oversee the Michelin-starred **Roca Moo** (see page 121), and their Midas touch extends to operatic food combinations at **Opera Samfaina** (see page 53) and gastronomic ice-creams at **Rocambolesc** (see page 58).

Vegetarians and vegans are also well-catered for in Barcelona, a highlight being **Green Spot** in Barceloneta (see page 92). Chef Teresa Carles specialises in healthy and sustainable takes on Catalan cuisine in her restaurants including the flexitarian **Flax & Kale** (see page 129), which features an 80 percent plant-based menu – the remaining 20 percent being fish.

... HOTEL HEAVEN

Barcelona is the design city *par excellence* and its hotels keep the theme going. **Hotel Omm** (see page 123) stands its own ground amid L'Eixample Modernista gems – its angled-window exterior by architect Juli Capella is a futuristic retake on the Casa Milà–La Pedrera and its black leather and wood interior, all light and minimalist lines, is very slick indeed. Then there's the jazz sessions at the hotel's Roca Bar (see page 117), Michelin eats at Roca Moo (see page 121) and ultimate pampering at its garden-hemmed Spaciomm spa.

A stay at the **W Barcelona** (see page 93) means unsurpassed views. The rooms are designer hubs filled with funky furnishings, wild Daliesque splashes and enormous picture windows framing in the sea. Those vistas are outshone only by the 'haute tapas' served at Carles Abellan's BRAVO24 in the 26th-floor Eclipse cocktail bar, or a luxury pampering session at its Bliss Spa.

Forty-four storeys of blue glass and exposed steel soaring high above the port of Vila Olímpica del Poblenou, the **Hotel Arts Barcelona** (see page 98) literally puts on the Ritz with plush rooms lapping up the marina location, a two Michelin-star modern Catalan kitchen, **Enoteca** (see page 105),

and insanely creative cocktails (see page 98).

The perfect mix of La Rambla streetlife and art, **Le Méridien** (see page 54) oozes mid-century flair. Some of its suites have outdoor rain showers from which you can survey the city's most famous boulevard. If you prefer a more intimate, bijou setting, opt for a stay in an apartment at **Barcino 147** (see page 115).

... A NIGHT ON THE TOWN

Given that Barcelona – along with the rest of Spain – only really starts to warm up for the night from 9pm onwards, finding something to do after dark is not a problem.

The stylish and upbeat **L'Eixample** has plenty of sleek after-work and pre-theatre cocktail bars (see page 117) with exquisite Modernista or neo-modernist decor. This vast neighbourhood also rounds up some of the city's best live jazz and blues spots within its six barrios.

Other neighbourhoods with top bar scenes are **El Raval**, which has a flurry of Barcelona-style gin bars (see page 50) ranging from the historic to the hip, and the carefree promenades and squares of **El Born** and **Sant Pere-Santa Caterina** (see page 71) whose terraces buzz into the early hours.

Gràcia is the hub of bohemian bars and vermouth sipping (see page 146) while **Port Vell**'s (see page 92) and **Barceloneta**'s (see page 86) beachfront bars combine beachy glamour with jaw-dropping views.

In keeping with its post-industrial experimental flair, the **El Poblenou** district is home to legendary multi-club music venue **Razzmatazz** (see page 109), where you can party and dance all night, listen to local and international performers or just chill.

If it's more an evening of classical music you are after head to the **Palau de la Música Catalana** (see page 67) or the **Liceu** (see page 58) for opera.

In summer the city's gardens and parks, including those in **La Ribera**, **Montjuïc** and **L'Eixample**, light up with various free concerts, from solo classical performances and orchestras to jazz and flamenco (see page 128).

... BEING SPORTY

The sea makes for a most scenic backdrop to a run or cycle ride. The waterfront stretch from the **Plaça del Mar**, by the landmark W Barcelona hotel in **Barceloneta** (see page 93), through to the **Parc del Fòrum** of **El Poblenou** (see page 106) is the city's most extraordinary outdoor exercise strip.

The series of seaside promenades – **Passeig Marítim** – feature wide bike and pedestrian lanes, alongside parkland, state-of-the-art skate-board parks (see page 107) as well as beachside workout zones (see page 93).

Major parks such as **La Ciutadella** (see page 68) are great for city sport aficionados with a choice of jogging and bike trails. You can also don your hiking shoes and head up to **Montjuïc hill** (see page 158) or **Park Güell** (see page 143) for an invigorating walk.

... LITERARY HAUNTS

The British novelist George Orwell is remembered as a hero in Catalonia for his involvement in the 1936 Spanish Civil War fighting alongside the Republicans. Most of Orwell's life in Barcelona centred on **La Rambla**, particularly in the area around the **Plaça de Catalunya**. From the **Hotel Continental** (138), where he stayed in 1937 and penned much of his *Homage to Catalonia* (1938), down to the **Liceu** opera house (see page 58) and the **Basílica de Santa Maria del Pi,** where he observed crowds running from bullets fired by youth anarchists. Opposite is the **Boqueria** market (see page 47) where he would refuel his way through fighting on a wedge of goat's milk cheese, or on an espresso from the now completely modernised Café Moka (126). You can book a **Civil War tour** to put Orwell's experience into context (see page 160).

A more recent novel featuring the city during the Civil War years is the bestselling Gothic literary thriller *The Shadow of the Wind* (2001), by Catalan Carlos Ruiz Zafón. Mostly set in **Barri Gòtic**, the Plaça Reial features prominently (see page 37).

Non-fiction musts are Robert Hughes' 1992 travelogue *Barcelona* and Colm Tóibín's 2002 *Homage to Barcelona*.

... NATURE

With over 90 parks, Barcelona is
a nature lover's idyllic city. Hilltop
Montjuïc alone has no less than 21,
including the vast **Parc de Montjuïc**,
the old amusement park, **Jardins de
Joan Brossa** (see page 154), and the
Jardins del Mirador de l'Alcalde with
its incredible lookout (see page 158).

Every neighbourhood has its green
spaces, some filled with sculptures
or Gaudí fountains. At one end of
the garden spectrum is the genteel,
historic **Parc de la Ciutadella** in
La Ribera (see page 68) and at the
other Jean Nouvel's contemporary
Parc del Centre del Poblenou
(see page 104) and the twisty-bendy
Parc de la Diagonal Mar (see page
101) on the waterfront.

... RETAIL THERAPY

High-heeled fashionistas revere
the **Passeig de Gràcia** in L'Eixample, lined with designer shops and
Barcelona-born retailers (see page
129). Running parallel, the **Rambla
de Catalunya** boasts mid-scale but
still refined shopping options.

For more affordable elegance,
head to Barri Gòtic's pedestrianised
Avinguda del Portal de l'Àngel.

Vintage, mod, artisan – the boutiques of **El Born** are colourful and
individualistic (see page 64) while
those in **El Raval** are more artistic
and cultural. And **Gràcia** is the home
of eco fashion and small clothing
and footwear ateliers (see page 140).

17

... ARCHITECTURE

Modernisme is Barcelona's great contribution to architecture. Colourful and flamboyant, the architectural and artistic style emerged around the time of the 1888 Universal Exhibition held in the Parc de la Ciutadella. Barcelona's 19th-century expansion (L'Eixample) gave Antoni Gaudí and his Modernista contemporaries the freedom and space to experiment. And nowhere does the movement reach more fantastical proportions than in Gaudí's still unfinished basilica **La Sagrada Família** (see page 130). The Gaudí trail continues to **Park Güell** (see page 143) and the private mansions and palaces of **Casa Vicens** (see page 144) in Gràcia and **Casa Milà** and **Battló** in L'Eixample, to the **Palau Güell** (see page 54) in El Raval.

Barcelona is just as good on the contemporary scene, with Jean Nouvel's **Torre Agbar** (see page 108), Enric Miralles' visionary sustainable sculptural design in the **Parc de Diagonal Mar**, and many more recent highlights in El Poblenou, literally the 'new town' (see page 100).

Architectural buffs will also want to visit the art nouveau **Mercat Sant Antoni** (see page 120), the **Palau de la Música** (see page 67) and Mies van der Rohe's iconic **Barcelona Pavilion** in Montjuïc (see page 161), built for the 1929 Universal Exhibition.

... STREET LIFE

Barcelona's main avenue, **La Rambla** (see page 38), is perpetually busy with tourists and vendors plying their wares. But to mingle with locals rather than tourists you need to head to the markets. Off La Rambla is the world-famous **Mercat de La Boqueria** (see page 47), and nearby are the **Mercat de la Concepció** (see page 126) and the **Mercat de Sant Antoni** (see page 120). In L'Eixample you have the **Mercat del Ninot** (see page 120), and in La Ribera the place to be is the **Mercat de Santa Caterina** (see page 71). In Gràcia the **Mercat de la Llibertat** (see page 147) also puts on folkloric street festivals (see page 141), which tap into the life and soul of the neighbourhood.

... ROMANCE

The beachfront and the old port are most romantic by night. Stroll the Barceloneta boardwalks and Passeig Marítim around the docks of **Port Vell** (see page 89), under the Gaudí streetlamps on the **Plaça Reial** (see page 37), or on the evocative cobblestones of **Barri Gòtic** (see page 32). The promenades and parks of the **Vila Olímpica** are much quieter and very atmospheric under the balmy moonlight (see page 104). The more adventurous romantics should head up to **Montjuïc's mirador** (see page 158) or even further afield to the **Bunkers del Carmel** (see page 136) for a hilltop view over the city.

NEIGHBOURHOODS

Barcelona radiates out from the waterfront and the Ciutat Vella (Old Town) to new-town areas such as L'Eixample, which shot up in the 19th century, and further north to former rural villages such as Gràcia in the hilly uptown. The districts of La Rambla, Barri Gòtic and El Raval together with Barceloneta, Port Vell and La Ribera, make up the historic nucleus of the city.

Barri Gòtic. This is the historical heart of the Old Town, built on top of the ancient Roman city of Barcino. As its name suggests this quarter packs in many Gothic treasures, including the Cathedral of Saint Eulalia and Gothic-Renaissance stately buildings in the Plaça Sant Jaume. The medieval walls marking the old city limits are no more, but now La Rambla demarcates Barri Gòtic to the west.

El Raval. The contemporary culture hub of the city, El Raval has a bold, fun and experimental feel. A mere rural village in the 10th century, the barrio evolved to become the cradle of the Industrial Revolution in 19th-century Spain. Still looking forward with feisty social innovation, it hinges on its contemporary arts and cultural institutions around the Plaça dels Àngels.

La Ribera and El Born. Sant Pere, Santa Caterina i la Ribera developed in the eastern part of the Old Town as medieval Barcelona expanded outside the Roman precinct. Its seafaring tradition lingers on in the hip barrio of El Born closest to the port, from the Plaça Comercial's old marketplace, through the bars and boutiques of the Passeig del Born, to the maritime church of Santa Maria del Mar. The narrow, winding streets of Sant Pere and Santa Caterina retain a strong medieval feel.

Barceloneta and Port Vell. The most youthful district of the Old Town, Barceloneta sprung up in the mid-18th century, when its narrow rows of workers' houses rehoused displaced residents from the La Ribera district that was being rebuilt. They later became home to fishermen, sailors and dockers and today it's more cafés, bodegas and shops. The village squares and markets retain a charming old-world ambience, distinct from the neon-lit docks and restaurants of Port Vell.

Vila Olímpica and El Poblenou. Sweeping along the coastline, taking in Barcelona's beaches and wide coastal boardwalks developed for the 1992 Olympic Games, the Vila Olímpica del Poblenou brought a new lease of life to a former industrial area. Sculptures, parklands, recreational facilities and dazzling architecture liven up the marina of Port Olímpic and beaches of Bagatell and Mar Bella, while the old textile factories of El Poblenou are morphing into spectacular skyscrapers, Torre Agbar shining bright amongst them.

L'Eixample. The fruit of Ildefons Cerdà's dramatic redesign of Barcelona in the 1860s, the 'expansion's' grid of elegant wide avenues became the perfect showcase for Modernista architecture, including the most imposing of all: Gaudí's masterpiece La Sagrada Família. It's also home to the elegant Passeig de Gràcia and numerous beautiful shops and Michelin restaurants.

Gràcia and beyond. Ask a local here where they're from and they will tell you they are from Gràcia, not Barcelona. An independent village until 1897, it was swallowed up with the expansion of L'Eixample but yet preserves a maverick charm, underpinned by a community of young bohemians, artists and students. Distance from the city centre is also a factor – Gràcia's five barrios extend into hillside La Salut, once home to a few scattered farmhouses, and now the realm of Park Güell.

Sants and Montjuïc. Bound by mountain and sea, with Montjuïc hill as its sentinel, the district south of the Ciutat Vella gathers in the city's most glorious parks and gardens, old villages such as El Poble Sec, treasure troves of ancient art, and emblematic Modernista landmarks built to show off Barcelona's architectural might to the world in the late 1920s.

Tibidabo ▲
512
VALLVIDRERA

NOU
BARRIS
HORTA-
GUINARDÓ
SANT-
ANDREU
Badalona

PARK GÜELL

Monestir
de Pedralbes
PEDRALBES

SARRIÀ-
SANT-GERVASI
GRACIA

LES CORTS

Cornellà de
Llobregat

L'Hospitalet
de Llobregat

SANT
MARTÍ

EIXAMPLE

C.VELLA

Barcelona

SANTS-
MONTJUÏC

Greater Barcelona

0   5 km
0   3 miles

N

L'Illa

Plaça
Doctor Ignacio
Barraquer

Plaça de
Francesc
Macià

NOVA ESQUERRA DE
L'EIXAMPLE

HOSTAFRANCS

LA BORDETA

PARC DE
JOAN MIRÓ

Plaça
Espanya

Arenas de
Barcelona

LA FONT DE LA GUATLLA

Fira de
Barcelona

SANT ANTONI

Caixa
Forum

Poble
Espanyol

Palau de
Congressos

Palau de
Victòria
Eugènia

Font
Màgica

Palau
d'Alfons
XIII

Mercat de
Sant Antoni

SANTS-
MONTJUÏC

Palau Nacional
Museu Nacional
d'Art de
Catalunya

EL POBLE SEC

Museu
d'Arqueologia

Open Camp

JARDINS DE
JOAN MARAGALL

Palau
Sant Jordi

Estadi
Olímpic

Fundació
Joan Miró

Sant P
del Car

Muntanya de

Montjuïc

PARC DE MONTJUÏC

Parc de Montjuïc

JARDINS
DE MOSSÈN
CINTO
VERADAGUER

MONTJUÏC

FOSSAR DE LA
PEDRERA

JARDÍ
BOTÀNIC

Plaça de
l'Armada

CEMENTIRI DE MONTJUÏC

Castell de
Montjuïc

Plaça de la Mirador

Transbordador A

Barcelona

0   500   1000 m
0   500   1000 yds

GRÀCIA

VILA DE GRÀCIA

EL CAMP D'EN GRASSOT I GRÀCIA NOVA

Plaça del Gal.la Placidia

Recinte Modernista de Sant Pau

SAGRADA FAMÍLIA

Casa Comalat

NTIGA ESQUERRA DE L'EIXAMPLE

Palau Robert

Palau Baró de Quadras

Casa de les Punxes

Casa Milà - La Pedrera

Palau Casades

Casa Thomas

Palau Montaner

Casa Elizalde

Fundació Antoni Tàpies

Palau Macaya

Plaça de la Sagrada Família

Sagrada Família

Plaça de Gaudí

Casa Batlló

Casa Amatller

Concepció

Mercat Concepció

Plaça de Pablo Neruda

Casa Lleó Morera

DRETA DE L'EIXAMPLE

EIXAMPLE

Plaça de Toros Monumental

Universitat Central

Plaça de la Universitat

Plaça de Tetuan

Plaça de les Glòries Catalanes

Plaça de Catalunya

El Corte Inglés

Mercat dels Encants

Museu del Disseny de Barcelona

Teatre Nacional de Catalunya

EL FORT PIENC

L'Auditori de Barcelona

MACBA

Casa de la Misericòrdia

Estació d'Autobusos del Nord

SANT MARTÍ

EL RAVAL

Palau Moja

Palau de la Virreina

Mercat de la Boqueria (Sant Josep)

Museu del Calçat

Catedral

Palau de la Música Catalana

Arc de Triomf

SANT PERE

Mercat Santa Caterina

EL PARC I LA LLACUNA DEL POBLENOU

Gran Teatre del Liceu

BARRI GÒTIC

SANTA CATERINA

LA RIBERA

Museu Picasso

PARC DE LA CIUTADELLA

Palau Güell

CIUTAT VELLA

Santa Maria del Mar

Mercat del Born

Plaça d'Armes

LA VILA OLÍMPICA DEL POBLENOU

EL BORN

Museu de la Cera

Llotja

Parlament de Catalunya

useu arítim

Mirador de Colom (Columbus Monument)

Estació de França

PARC ZOOLÒGIC (ZOO)

VILA OLÍMPICA

Museu d'Història de Catalunya

PARC DEL PORT OLÍMPIC

Port Vell

BARCELONETA

Església de Sant Miquel del Port

L'Aquàrium

Marina Port Vell

Torre de les Aigües

Torre Mapfre

Maremàgnum

Mercat de Barceloneta

PARC DE LA BARCELONETA

Port Olímpic

Platja de Nova Icària

World rade enter

Platja de la Barceloneta

Platja de la Barceloneta

BARRI GÒTIC

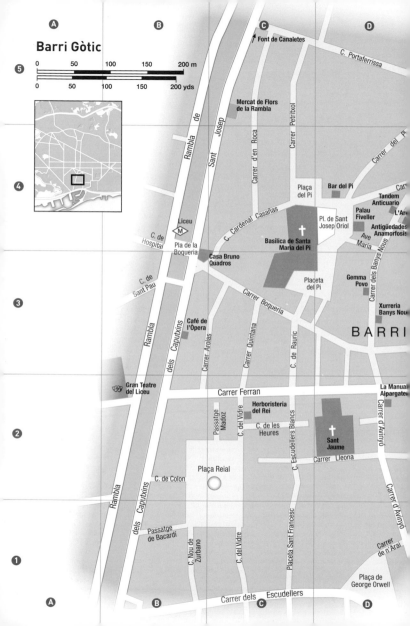

Barri Gòtic

0 50 100 150 200 m
0 50 100 150 200 yds

Font de Canaletes
C. Portaferrissa
Mercat de Flors de la Rambla
Carrer Petritxol
Carrer d'en Roca
Rambla de Sant Josep
Carrer del Pi
Plaça del Pi
Bar del Pi
Tandem Anticuario
L'Ar
Palau Fiveller
Pl. de Sant Josep Oriol
Antigüedades Anamorfosis
C. Cardenal Casañas
Basílica de Santa Maria del Pi
Ave Maria
Liceu
Pla de la Boqueria
C. de Hospital
Casa Bruno Quadros
Gemma Povo
Placeta del Pi
Carrer dels Banys Nous
C. de Sant Pau
Carrer Boqueria
Xurreria Banys Nou
Rambla
dels Caputxins
Café de l'Òpera
Carrer Arolas
Carrer Quintana
C. de Rauric
BARRI
Gran Teatre del Liceu
Carrer Ferran
La Manual Alpargate
Carrer d'Avinyó
Passatge Madoz
C. del Vidre
Herboristeria del Rei
C. de les Heures
C. Escudellers Blancs
Sant Jaume
Carrer Lleona
C. de Colon
Plaça Reial
Carrer d'Avinyó
Passatge de Bacardi
C. Nou de Zurbano
C. del Vidre
Placeta Sant Francesc
Carrer de n'Arai
Plaça de George Orwell
Carrer dels Escudellers

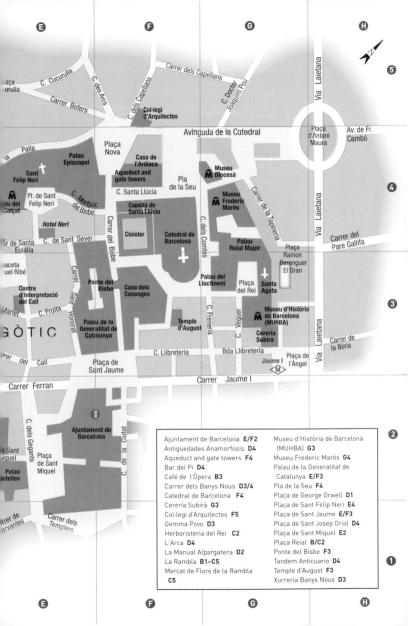

E F G H

5

C. Cucurulla
aça
curulla
C. des Arcs
Carrer Boters
C. dels Capellans
Carrer dels Capellans
C. Doctor Joaquim Pou
Via Laietana
Col·legi d'Arquitectes
Avinguda de la Catedral
Plaça d'Antoni Maura
Av. de Fr. Cambó

4

la Palla
Palau Episcopal
Sant Felip Neri
eu del Calçat
Pl. de Sant Felip Neri
Hotel Neri
C. Montjuic del Bisbe
C. de Sant Sever
a de Santa Eulàlia
Plaça Nova
Casa de l'Ardiaca
Aqueduct and gate towers
C. Santa Llúcia
Capella de Santa Llúcia
Cloister
Carrer del Bisbe
Pla de la Seu
Museu Diocesà
Museu Frederic Marès
Catedral de Barcelona
C. dels Comtes
Palau Reial Major
Carrer de la Tapineria
Plaça Ramon Berenguer El Gran
Via Laietana
Carrer del Pare Gallifa

3

aceta uel Ribé
Centre d'Interpretació del Call
Marlet
C. Fruita
GÒTIC
Ponte del Bisbe
Casa dels Canonges
Carrer Sant Honorat
Palau de la Generalitat de Catalunya
Temple d'August
Palau del Lloctinent
C. Freneria
Plaça del Rei
Santa Agata
Veguer
Museu d'Història de Barcelona (MUHBA)
Cereria Subirà
Via Laietana
Carrer de la Bòria

2

rer del Call
Plaça de Sant Jaume
C. Llibreteria
Bda Llibreteria
Plaça de l'Àngel
Jaume I
M

Carrer Ferran
Carrer Jaume I

C. dels Gegants
Ajuntament de Barcelona
C. de la Ciutat
a Sant quel
Plaça de Sant Miquel
Palau ntelles
Carrer de ervantes
Carrer dels Templers

Get the vintage vibe while eating the best churros in the city on Carrer dels Banys Nous

Barcelona is a city of mini neighbourhoods within neighbourhoods, often clustered around just one street. **Carrer dels Banys Nous** (map D3/4) is one of them. The name, 'new baths', refers to the medieval Jewish baths built here just outside the ancient Roman walls, whose path it traces in a graceful sweep. This is antiques street, lined as it is with quaint, immaculately groomed antique shops. **Tandem Anticuario** (19; map D4) has a lot of coloured glass, ceramics and porcelain as well as paintings and objets d'art from around the world.

L'Arca (20; map D4) is Spanish for nuptial trunk, so you'll find here exquisite vintage wedding dresses, floral headpieces and period clothing: 1920s flapper dresses, vintage Japanese kimonos, fur collars and geometric prints as well as international creations from the likes of Dior, Yves Saint-Laurent, Hermès and Chanel, and Spanish designers Balenciaga and Pedro Rodríguez y Asunción Bastida.

A third-generation interior design business founded in 1953, **Gemma Povo** (5–7; map D3) showcases an unusual mix of custom-made lighting, furniture and fashion by artisan woodworkers, ironmongers, glassworkers and screen makers. Their iron lamps for floor, wall, table and ceiling have classical forms with contemporary twists such as bright silk shades.

Tucked away in a tiny alley off Carrer dels Banys Nous, **Antigüedades Anamorfosis** (Baixada de Santa Eulàlia, 4; map D4) has an incredible, personally curated collection of vintage radios and phonographs, all restored and functioning perfectly.

For some mid-shopping nourishment stop at **Xurreria Banys Nous** (8; map D3), whose churros are regularly rated among the city and country's best. There's no sitting space, so just grab a cone of the doughy delights and keep on window shopping.

Shop back in time in Barcelona's oldest commercial establishments

The exquisite dollhouse shop front of **Cerería Subirà** (Baixada de la Llibreteria, 7; map G3), with its pink satin-draped displays of candles and jewellery, belies its history as Barcelona's first ever shopping establishment. Manufacturing candles since 1761, the shop resembles a mini Versailles with panelled interiors of pale green and yellow *boiserie* bearing ornamental carvings, and flame-carrying voluptuous female statues guarding a symmetrical sweep of wood-railed stairways leading to an upper gallery. Myriad coloured candles and more classical church and taper styles are on display in its period cabinets.

From old wax to medicinal plants, the **Herboristeria del Rei** (Carrer del Vidre, 1; map C2) is another of the city's oldest businesses, established in 1818 and now a listed building. In a surprisingly lookalike shop though far more fussy in decoration, here the architectural influence is Elizabethan. When Queen Isabel II gave the shop a royal warrant in 1857, the premises were promptly renovated by renowned painter and theatrical set designer Francesc Soler Rovirosa. In the midst of all the lavish wood mouldings, watercolour-painted cabinet drawers and glass ceiling is a Carrara-marble fountain that once stocked curative leeches; it's topped with the bust of Carl Von Linné, the Swedish botanist often recognised as the father of taxonomy. This treasure trove of herbs and spices, honey and tea, and decorative glass containers, even has a little art gallery upstairs. The current owner is a master herbalist, recognised as such by the Catalan Government, so you know you are in safe hands here.

Artisan espadrilles

For a complete departure from vintage, yet sticking to fine manufacturing traditions, follow the likes of Penélope Cruz, Michael Douglas – and Salvador Dalí before them – to **La Manual Alpargatera** (Carrer d'Avinyó, 7; www.lamanualalpargatera.es; map D2), for eco-friendly yet very on-trend espadrilles.

29

Meet the geese in the exquisite cloister of the Gothic Cathedral

The divinely mish-mash **Catedral de Barcelona** (map F4) – or Catedral de la Santa Creu i Santa Eulàlia to use its official name – was six centuries in the making starting from 1298. Possibly outshining the cathedral's impressive interior though are the cloisters, a quiet haven away from the crowds and heat made up of pretty fountains and a romantic garden of palms, fruit trees and intensely fragranced magnolia trees where an endearing population of 13 geese roam about freely. Do not underestimate the appeal of these creatures, for animal lovers, children and those partial to some good storytelling.

Legends about the origins and meaning of the 13 honking birds abound. Some say the number symbolises the age in centuries of the cathedral's foundation stones, others believe it refers to the age of Saint Eulàlia, co-patron saint of Barcelona, when she died. An even more gruesome account puts is down to the number of tortures the saint supposedly suffered during the persecution of Christians by Romans in the reign of Emperor Diocletian. Whatever their significance, their loud cackling can be heard throughout the cathedral, and in the past it acted as an alarm bell against intruders and thieves.

Bop with buskers or forage for flea market finds on the Pla de la Seu

The mighty Catedral de Barcelona is a communal vision shared by all on the **Pla de la Seu** (map F4), the most uplifting city square.

Festivities, protests, public art and music animate this meeting place day and night. The *Pla* is actually another pet name for the Cathedral, *La Seu*, meaning the bishop's see or seat.

This is a square where the saying 'all the world's a stage' rings true. Crowds flood the stairs unfurling to the front of the Holy Cross and Saint Eulàlia, which is crowned with ornately carved figurines and metal spires, and listen to the buskers who regularly perform here. Take shade under the olive trees out front and soak in the atmosphere. It's a very infectious public mood which grips the throngs, all this played out against the surprisingly neo-Gothic front of the cathedral, whose two octagonal towers are set within the former boundary of the ancient Roman city.

On Thursdays from 10am to 8pm the stage transforms into a bric-a-brac market, the **Mercat Gotic de Antiguidades**. Antique aficionados and collectors rummage through the stalls piled with candelabras, jewellery, watches,

silverware, coins, postcards, embroidery and other relics at this long-running antiques market skirting the **Avinguda de la Catedral**. This could be your chance to buy a vintage Spanish lace shawl or fan. Prices here reflect the quality of the items on sale, but you'll also find the usual trinkets that make for perfect souvenirs.

Get lost in a cobblestoned labyrinth and sip coffee in revolutionary surroundings

The Barri Gòtic is a honeycomb of small narrow streets linking small medieval squares *(placetas)* to grand Renaissance ones. Great joy lies in strolling leisurely from one to another, discovering the delightful surprises that lie at each corner.

Along from the Catedral via the tiny little Carrer del Paradis you come to the handsome **Plaça de Sant Jaume** (map E/F3). It is the civic heart of the city, home on one side to the neoclassical **Ajuntament de Barcelona** (1; map E/F2), the City Council, and the **Palau de la Generalitat de Catalunya** (4; map E/F3), the seat of the government of Catalonia and as such guarded by the Mossos d'Esquadra, the autonomous police force. The palace was built over the 15th and 17th centuries; its two side facades are Gothic while the front one was added later, inspired by Rome's Renaissance Palazzo Farnese and featuring a statue of St George on its balcony.

Leaving from the south-western corner of the square you will find yourself in the **Plaça de Sant Miquel**

(map E2) confronted by an unusual towering wire sculpture. The *Monumento a los Castellers* pays homage to the human towers, *castellers*, built during Catalan festivals by people standing on each other's shoulders.

A five-minute stroll north takes you to the delightful **Plaça de Sant Felip Neri** (map E4), a small square enclosed by heavy stone buildings and happily neglected, which only adds to its charm. It is presided over by the little Baroque church of the same name. For all its romance, a sombre past lurks.

A bomb dropped here in 1938 during the Civil War, killing 42 people, and the pockmarked church facade tells the tale.

Nearby shade can be found under the pines and plane trees of the **Plaça de Sant Josep Oriol** (map D4), dominated by the sought-after terrace of the **Bar del Pi** (1; map D4), an institution and the perfect place for a cup of coffee. Historic for more than its vintage mirrors and lights, this is where the anti-Fascist Unified Socialist Party of Catalonia was founded in July 1936.

Enter a time capsule at the Museu Frederic Marès

Over a lifetime spanning 98 years, Catalan sculptor Frederic Marès (1893–1991) amassed an incredible personal collection of religious art and artefacts, women's fashion and accessories, seashells, toy soldiers, medieval sculptures, jewellery, photographs, keys, pharmacy bottles and reliquaries. He bequeathed it to the city in 1946 and two years later the **Museu Frederic Marès** (map G4) opened its doors as the treasures kept rolling in.

Marès attended Barcelona's School of Fine Arts, La Llotja, almost at the same epoch as Picasso. He is known for his monumental sculptures, two of which – *Barcelona* and *Emporion* – grace the Plaça de Catalunya. Some of his personal works are on display here, and his large collection of mostly polychrome Spanish religious sculptures occupies the ground and first floors.

The 'Collector's Cabinet', spreading over the next two floors, is at the core of a more whacky and whimsical gathering of objects in themed rooms, including the Weapons Hall (old armours, swords and crossbows) and the Smoker's Hall (tobacco artefacts including elaborately carved pipes, etc)

People love the personal atmosphere of the museum, which in the Middle Ages was part of the Royal Palace quarters for the Counts of Barcelona. At the end of your journey back in time, make sure to visit the bucolic courtyard with its delightful fountain and orange trees. In summer its arched galleries shade the tables of the Cafè d'estiu.

Museu Frederic Marès; Plaça de Sant Lu, 5–6; tel: 932 563 500; Tue–Sat 10am–7pm, Sun 11am–8pm; http://w110.bcn.cat/ museufredericmares
Café; Apr–Sept, Tue–Sun 10am–10pm

Admire Picasso street art and browse for books at the Catalan College of Architects

What first hits you upon approaching the **Collegi d'Arquitectes de Catalunya** are the friezes of bullfighters and branch-carrying children adorning the front and right facades of the building. These were reproduced with painstaking precision from drawings done by Picasso in 1960, expressly to beautify the controversial structure. Inaugurated a few years earlier, its two superimposed concrete slabs stand at odds with the Gothic cathedral across the way and provoked considerable outcry at the time. And so, inspired by Miró's murals for the Unesco headquarters in Paris, the project's architectural director Xavier Busquets i Sindreu approached Picasso.

Picasso's series of drawings depicting Catalan festivals and folklore such as the *sardana* dance were recreated by the Norwegian artist Carl Nesjar, first by projecting them on paper from several meters away to get the required scale, then fixing the painted papers on the concrete panels, perforating them with holes and sandblasting the silhouettes in order to make a precise simile of each line of Picasso's works, revealed in black stone. The trio of murals go with the names of 'children's frieze', 'giants' frieze' and 'frieze of the Catalan flag'.

There's also interest inside the building: in the basement the centre's bookshop is a treasure-trove of tomes on urban design and interiors and there are also gifts, paper, and even graphic design tools and equipment for sale.

Collegi d'Arquitectes de Catalunya;
Plaça Nova, 5; tel: 34 93 301 50 00;
www.arquitectes.cat; map F5
Librería La Capell; Mon–Fri 9am–2.30pm
& 5–7pm

Duck the evil eye under the Bishop's Bridge

Strolling along the Carrer del Bisbe towards the cathedral, look up to the **Pont del Bisbe**, the intricately carved stone bridge connecting the Casa dels Canonges, the old Canon's House – now the official residence of the Catalan President with the government seat and offices – with the Palau de la Generalitat.

Looking at it you would never guess the Pont del Bisbe was an afterthought. The 'Bishop's Bridge' was the work of architect Joan Rubió i Bellver, a Gaudí modernist contemporary who drew up a plan for a complete makeover of this pocket of the Barri Gòtic in 1927, to bring it into step with the neo-Gothic style of the day. His vision was rejected, other than this ornate bridge completed in 1927, which blends in seamlessly with the medieval surrounds.

Rubió sought revenge in a cheeky way, implanting a sword-pierced skull in the footbridge facade. As you pass underneath, perhaps avoid direct eye contact with the skull and dagger protruding from its mouth. According to legend, that will bring you bad luck. Others believe the opposite however, so you can take a gamble. But whatever you do, don't remove it – another tale predicts that would lead to the fall of Barcelona.

Ponte del Bisbe; map F3

Jazz it up or flamenco the night away in the Plaça Reial

Just off the Rambla with arcades opening onto the Gothic quarter on three sides, the harmoniously rectilinear **Plaça Reial** is one of Barcelona's most handsome squares.

Inspired by the French urban designs of the Napoleonic period, the handsome girth of late 19th-century neoclassical residences with their tiny balconies and terracotta frills are offset by equally symmetrical sweeps of arches. The square's architect set out to immortalise King Ferdinand VII with an equestrian statue but instead the square is graced by a wrought-iron *Fountain of the Three Graces*, now the focal point of a stamp and coin market on Sunday mornings. The two street lamps flanking the fountain, surmounted by a winged helmet and dragon, were designed by a young Gaudí in 1879. Handsome, mature palm trees add to the elegance of the surroundings.

Once home to a medieval Capuchin convent, the square now buzzes with street life, with a variety of buskers vying to entertain the many tourists. Under the arches, restaurants, bars and clubs predominate, mostly geared to tourists but it is worth the extra cash to enjoy the glorious setting with a drink or seafood meal. And the entertainment continues in the well-established **Jamboree** jazz club (17), along with its sister club **Tarantos** for flamenco, both open after the shows for dancing the night away.

Plaça Reial; map B/C2

Go with the flow on one of the world's greatest show-off strips

La Rambla is one of the most famous boulevards in Europe. From the Plaça de Catalunya all the way down to the waterfront, Barcelona's main pedestrian street unfurls over 1.5km (1 mile) taking in five mini-Ramblas: **Ramblas de Caneletes**, **dels Estudis**, **de Sant Josep**, **dels Caputxins** and **de Santa Mònica**.

La Rambla started as a waterway (*rambla* comes from the Arabic *ramla*, meaning 'sandy riverbed'). Water once flowed down here from the mountains above, canalised by fortified towers on the Rambla de Caneletes. The riverbed lay just outside the city walls built in the 13th and 14th centuries, but was filled in with the demolition of the walls four centuries later. That's when the boulevard slowly came to life, as the fashionable hub of a budding city. It experienced its heyday in the 18th century as a gardened boulevard of banks, shops, theatres, hotels, restaurants and markets.

Now, it's a constant stream of people, both tourists and locals. The best advice is to plunge in, go with the flow and enjoy the constant weird and wonderful activity. Watch out for pickpockets though, as they inevitably prey on such a bountiful crowd. Join the buzzing throng on La Rambla's upper stretch, watching out for the **Font de Canaletes** fountain. Local lore says first-time Barcelona visitors who drink from the urn-shaped iron font, fall in love with the city and are sure to return. These days it's a gathering place for Barcelona Football Club fans – a tradition dating to the pre-internet 1930s when *La Rambla* newspaper gave out match results on a nearby blackboard.

In the 19th century, La Rambla had become the preferred meeting place for the aristocracy. They flocked to the flower and bird kiosks

Rambla street art

The colourful and extravagant **Casa Bruno Cuadros** on the Rambla Sant Josep (La Rambla, 82; map B3) is a showcase for the Modernistas' penchant for Oriental decorations. In 1883 architect Josep Vilaseca embellished the house with sgraffito work, stained-glass windows, intricate carpentry, balconies embellished with Egyptian imagery, cast-iron reliefs of umbrellas and fans, paintings of figurines from Japanese prints and a great Chinese dragon. This show-stopper is nicknamed 'the umbrella house', *Casa dels Paraigües*, in memory of the old umbrella shop that once graced the ground floor. Nearby is Joan Miró's unmissable moon-shaped 1976 pavement mosaic, ***Pla de l'Os***.

on the stroller's *paseo*, which is why Rambla dels Estudis and Rambla Sant Josep are respectively nicknamed Rambla dels Ocells and Rambla de les Flors. The latter section of La Rambla is still devoted to daily flower stalls, the **Mercat de Flors de la Rambla** (map C5). All the eastern sidewalks of the pedestrianised Rambla have today been swept into the Barri Gòtic, and its its western flanks into El Raval.

Further down towards the harbour, the Rambla del Capuxtins, also known as the Rambla del Centre, takes its name from a former convent of Capuchin friars. It boasts a cluster of some of the city's prettiest houses, heritage-listed noble residences and palaces with frescoed walls and ceilings, painted facades and wood embellishments. Among them is the **Cafè de l'Òpera** (map B3), once an 18th century coaching tavern and later a swish 19th-century *chocolatería*, before opening in its current guise in 1929. The establishment is still decorated in a Viennese style with wooden walls, chandeliers, gilded mirrors and classical paintings.

Your big rollicking ramble down La Rambla should wind up on the harbour side, at the Monument a Colom, the Columbus Monument. An internal lift takes you to the mirador, for a great view of the city and port.

La Rambla; map B1–5
Mirador de Colomb; daily 8.30am–8.30pm

39

Explore Barcelona's Roman past, when it was known as Barcino

As you eye up the city's Gothic cathedral from the Plaça Nova the drama of its spires rising theatrically above the Roman walls is a sight to behold.

Shouldering the Gothic masterpiece are the vestiges of an **aqueduct** and of an entrance **gate** (map F4), all part of the first walls built in the 4th century AD to protect the Roman city of Barcino that once occupied much of what is now the Barri Gòtic.

This and several other Roman relics are part of a 'Points of Historical Interest of Roman Barcelona' trail, numbered on copper-coloured signs, in this case "R | 12" as the Plaça Nova relics are the last in a loop taking in a dozen sites.

The itinerary was mapped out by MUHBA, the **Museu d'Història de Barcelona** (Plaça del Rei; http://museuhistoria.bcn.cat; map G3), which is one of the stops en route. The museum is housed in a

monumental archaeological site on the Plaça del Rei. The so-called **Yacimiento Arqueológico**, R | 1, is the kick-off point for Roman Barcelona. Here you can stroll through the subterranean excavated streets of Barcino and inside some of the buildings.

Next comes the **Temple d'August** (map F3) in Carrer Paradís (10), hidden away in a small medieval courtyard. Four mighty 9m (30 ft) -high columns and fragments of the transept and its plinth are all that survive of the 1st-century BC temple, dedicated to Rome's Emperor at the time, Augustus. The original temple was 37m (121 ft) long and 17m (55 ft) wide, with six frontal columns (hexastyle). The temple was reconstructed by the famous Modernista architect Puig i Cadafalch in the early 20th century.

'Paradise Street' is thought to be named after an ancient garden planted in the vicinity of the shrine. A milestone opposite the temple marks the highest point of the Roman city, **Mont Tàber**, a mere 16m (52 ft) -high hillock.

Other stops along the Roman trail include a Roman tower on the Plaça dels Traginers and more of the Roman wall and defence towers on the Plaça Ramon Berenguer.

Be a true Catalan and dance the *sardana* on a balmy summer night

While Barcelona does have places to watch and learn flamenco, the only true culturally appropriate dance here is *la sardana*, Catalonia's national dance, which returned with a vengeance after decades of Franco repression.

Dating from as early as the 16th century, in its present form it grew out of the early 19th-century *Renaixença*, when Catalans rediscovered their cultural identity. You will be able to feel the regional pride deeply rooted in this dance, which is an integral part of Catalan culture and identity – no festival is complete without it.

The *sardana* is danced in a circle with dancers holding hands, bopping gently up and down to the tunes of a *cobla* band of flutes and oboes, dressed in black, white and red pants and skirts with matching espadrilles.

The intricate footwork apparently takes years to master but this is a social dance with bystanders encouraged to join in. You can learn a few steps during the weekend summer performances in front of the cathedral (Sat from 6pm, Sun 11.15am–1pm and Wed at 7pm) and on the Plaça de Sant Jaume (Sun 6pm), or during festivals such as La Mercè in September.

EL RAVAL

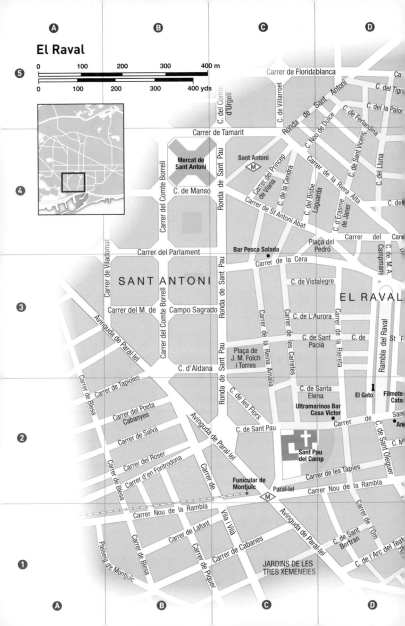

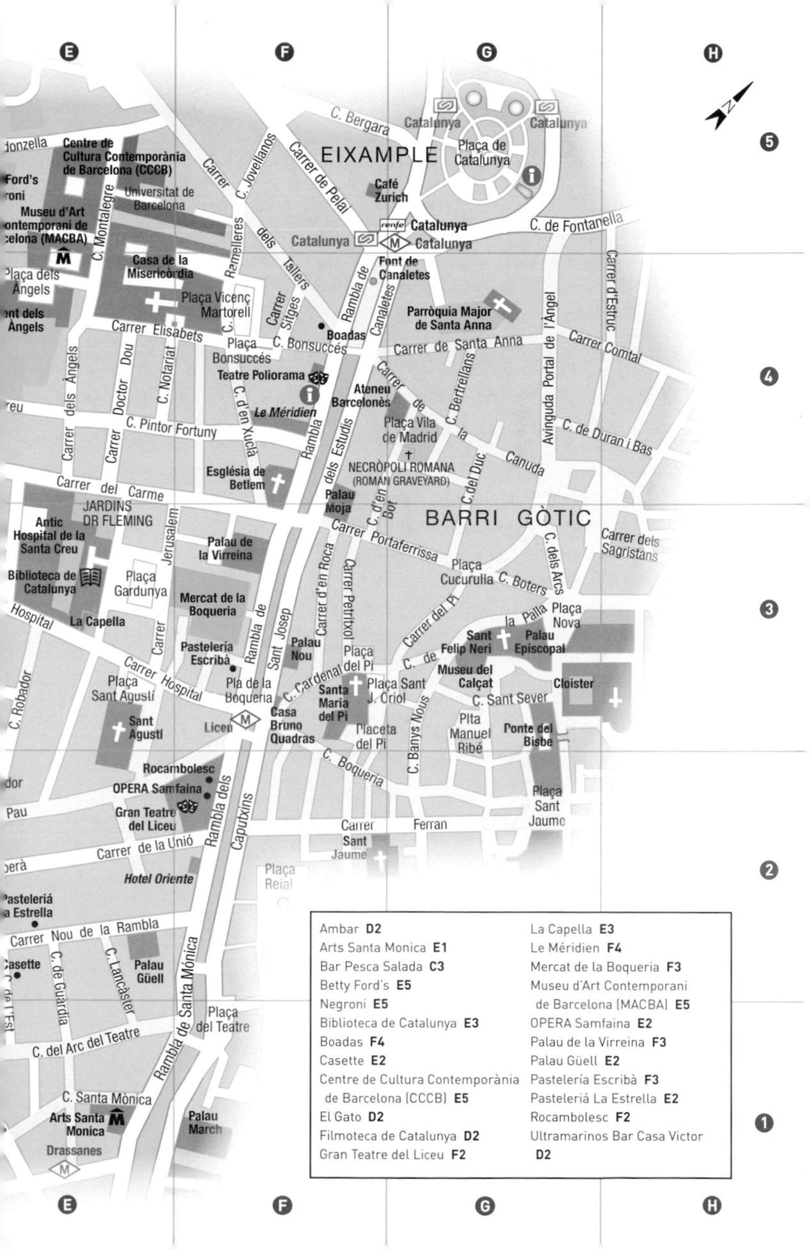
E
F
G
H
5
4
3
2
1
EIXAMPLE
BARRI GÒTIC
C. Bergara
Catalunya
Plaça de Catalunya
Carrer de Pelai
Café Zurich
renfe Catalunya
Catalunya
M Catalunya
C. de Fontanella
Carrer d'Estruc
Font de Canaletes
Rambla de Canaletes
Parròquia Major de Santa Anna
Avinguda Portal de l'Àngel
Carrer Comtal
Carrer de Santa Anna
C. Jovellanos
Carrer
Centre de Cultura Contemporània de Barcelona (CCCB)
Universitat de Barcelona
Museu d'Art Contemporani de Barcelona (MACBA)
C. Montalegre
Ramelleres
dels Tallers
Casa de la Misericòrdia
Plaça dels Àngels
Plaça Vicenç Martorell
Carrer Sitges
Boadas
Carrer Elisabets
Plaça Bonsuccés
C. Bonsuccés
Teatre Poliorama
Ateneu Barcelonès
Carrer de la Canuda
C. Bertrellans
C. de Duran i Bas
Carrer dels Àngels
Carrer Doctor Dou
C. Notariat
C. d'en Xuclà
Le Méridien
Rambla dels Estudis
Plaça Vila de Madrid
NECRÒPOLI ROMANA (ROMAN GRAVEYARD)
C. Pintor Fortuny
Església de Betlem
C. del Duc
Carrer del Carme
JARDINS DR FLEMING
Palau Moja
C. d'en Bot
Antic Hospital de la Santa Creu
Jerusalem
Palau de la Virreina
Carrer Portaferrissa
C. dels Arcs
Carrer dels Sagristans
Biblioteca de Catalunya
Plaça Gardunya
Carrer d'en Roca
Carrer Petritxol
Plaça Cucurulla
C. Boters
Mercat de la Boqueria
Hospital
La Capella
Carrer del Pi
la Palla
Plaça Nova
Rambla de Sant Josep
Palau Nou
Sant Felip Neri
Palau Episcopal
Pastelería Escribà
Carrer Hospital
Plaça del Pi
C. de
Museu del Calçat
Cloister
Plaça Sant Agustí
Pla de la Boqueria
C. Cardenal
Santa Maria del Pi
Plaça Sant J. Oriol
C. Sant Sever
C. Robador
Sant Agustí
Liceu
Casa Bruno Quadras
Placeta del Pi
C. Banys Nous
Plta Manuel Ribé
Ponte del Bisbe
C. Boqueria
Rocambolesc
OPERA Samfaina
Rambla dels Caputxins
Plaça Sant Jaume
Gran Teatre del Liceu
Carrer Ferran
Sant Jaume
Carrer de la Unió
Hotel Oriente
Plaça Reial
Pasteleriá La Estrella
Carrer Nou de la Rambla
Casette
C. de Guàrdia
C. Lancàster
Palau Güell
Rambla de Santa Mònica
Plaça del Teatre
C. del Arc del Teatre
C. Santa Mònica
Arts Santa Monica
Palau March
Drassanes

Ambar **D2**
Arts Santa Monica **E1**
Bar Pesca Salada **C3**
Betty Ford's **E5**
Negroni **E5**
Biblioteca de Catalunya **E3**
Boadas **F4**
Casette **E2**
Centre de Cultura Contemporània de Barcelona (CCCB) **E5**
El Gato **D2**
Filmoteca de Catalunya **D2**
Gran Teatre del Liceu **F2**
La Capella **E3**
Le Méridien **F4**
Mercat de la Boqueria **F3**
Museu d'Art Contemporani de Barcelona (MACBA) **E5**
OPERA Samfaina **E2**
Palau de la Virreina **F3**
Palau Güell **E2**
Pastelería Escribà **F3**
Pasteleriá La Estrella **E2**
Rocambolesc **F2**
Ultramarinos Bar Casa Victor **D2**

Follow the pink and blue pills into El Raval's arty underbelly

Many contemporary art spaces are clustered around the Rambla, especially on the El Raval side lending it a certain arty effervescence and irreverence.

These venues have been given more visibility by being featured on the **Circuit d'Art Contemporani**. This contemporary art route links art galleries, foundations, museums and centres via a series of coloured, pill-shaped waymarkers – pink for private galleries, blue for institutions – which are clearly labelled and numbered for convenience. There is also an online interactive map (www.artbarcelona.es/circuit), which allows you to beam up information on all the venues and their current exhibitions courtesy of Art Barcelona, Abe, a network of galleries devoted to contemporary art. The information also feeds into the mobile Barcelona Contactless platform via a smartphone and QR code so you can zip about paper-free.

As well as the contemporary arts museum MACBA (see page 56) and the contemporary cultural centre CCCB (see page 59), another highlight is the **Arts Santa Mònica** dedicated to digital culture. Its breezy location on the waterfront is reminiscent of its Los Angeles neighbourhood namesake. Contemporary, creative, cosmopolitan and free, its multidisciplinary exhibitions cover architecture, performing arts, visual arts, music, literature, design and gastronomy under thought-provoking titles such as AFTERMATH: Architecture Beyond Architects, or Decoding Zoom in Design.

Combining art and religious surroundings, **La Capella**, located in the chapel of the former Hospital de la Santa Creu, exposes the work of emerging artists in a beautiful long space of stone walls and white vaulted ceilings.

Arts Santa Mònica; La Rambla, 7;
tel: 935 671 110; Tue–Sat 11am–9pm,
Sun 11am–5pm; free; map E1
La Capella; Hospital, 56; Tue–Sat 12–8pm,
Sun 11am–2pm; map E3

Eat your way around the gastronomic temple of La Boqueria

Under a large iron-and-glass art nouveau roof, sprawls out Barcelona's most famous covered market, showcasing Catalonia's wide variety of produce from the mountains, rich farmlands and the sea.

Located on the El Raval side of La Rambla de Sant Josep, the medieval **Mercat de la Boqueria** started as a humble open-air farmer's market selling fruit and vegetables on the Pla de la Boqueria, in the shadow of one of the old city wall gates.

Times they are a-changing and in recent years tradition has given way to trend, with juice bars and fusion food. In 2016 the newspaper La Vanguardia called the market 'a gigantic take-away' referring to the way traders are adapting to tourist demands for on-the-go food: 'La Boqueria fishmongers are adding to the food rush with oysters ready to be swallowed, tiger prawns, battered fish, cod croquettes and assorted grilled seafood.'

While it is undeniably touristy, it is still an intoxicating experience, as there is something quintessentially Mediterranean about the noise, human warmth and eating wonderfully fresh produce. And if that was not enough praise, then you'll have to take Barcelona's famous chef

Ferran Adrià's – of former El Bulli fame – words for it: 'La Boqueria is a gastronomic temple, a place that congregates all the phases in the food chain, from the producers, harvesters, butchers and fishmongers, to the individuals and professionals who wander through this magnificent, characteristic maze of traders and market stalls.'

So get lost in the maze of market stalls then take a seat and savour some cooked-on-the-spot tapas, tortilla or the dish of the day with a glass of red at the legendary little **Pinotxo Bar** (Stall 466–470, daily 6.30am–4pm).

La Boqueria; La Rambla, 91; 8am–8.30pm; www.boqueria.info; map F3

Be uplifted by a Gothic read in the serenity of a cloister

Retreat to the peace, orange trees and fountains of the **Jardins de Rubió i Lluch**, a heavenly gardened cloister framed by the ancient stone walls of the **Biblioteca de Catalunya** and other chapels and buildings of the old Santa Creu hospital.

The glorious cross-vaulted ceilings of the Gothic library watch over three million books that are accessible to the public. And for several years running, the library has organised 'Llegim al jardí', Let's Read in the Garden, transforming the cloister into an exquisite outdoor reading place.

So make sure you have some ID with you and grab a book and a park bench, or an old pew in the shade of the massive arcades, and enjoy your read lulled by the refreshing breeze over the fountains. A book, magazine and newspaper loan service is also available, and you can be online outdoors with free Wi-Fi.

The library also provides plenty of information about the history and architecture of the hospital building, and botanical background on the trees and vegetation living in the gardens. And watch out for the concerts it organises, from soloist sopranos to piano recitals and cabaret.

*Biblioteca de Catalunya; Carrer de l'Hospital, 56; tel 93 270 2300; Mon–Fri 9am–8pm, Sat 9am–4pm; map E3
Let's Read in the Garden; 20 Mar–10 Nov Mon–Fri 10.30am–6pm*

Feast your eyes and your tummy at a Modernista chocolate shop

Walking down La Rambla towards the waterfront your eyes will be drawn to the elaborate shop front of **Escribà**. The famous pastry shop, or *pastelería*, is housed in the Antigua Casa Figueras, dating back to 1820. Its miniature glass-arched facade is splashed in sculptures, a peacock tail leadlight and mosaic flowers.

And if the exterior is not to your taste than let the waffles being served up from the street-opening stall tempt you inside. The wood-lined interior boasts gorgeously detailed painted ceilings and coloured glasswork but the real artistic treasures here are edible: fine chocolates and pastries fill the glass cabinets. Willy Wonka eat your heart out: the surreal selection includes everything from red Warhol lips filled with ganache, sunglass-wearing elfins and a chocolate Eiffel Tower.

Founded in 1906, the family-owned store gained world renown when Antoni Escribá, the 'chocolate sculptor', took over, making choc-olate eggs for the likes of Salvador Dalí and Picasso. His son Christian lives up to his father's legacy and his award-winning chocolate shoes and signature Candy-Glam rings have featured in high-end Parisian department stores window displays.

Be tempted by a giant-sized *ensaïmada*. The fluffy pastry coils dusted in icing sugar are more a Balearic tradition, but their name derives from the Catalan word *saim* for lard (though butter is more often used nowadays). Sometimes filled with preserves or cream, those at Escribà are plain, and simply divine.

Escribà's motto is 'We do not just make cakes, we make illu-sions'. Thankfully their chocolate creations are real and you can buy small boxes to take home.

Pastelería Escribà, La Rambla 83; tel: 93 301 60 27; map F3

Bar-hop Barcelona's hottest gin bars

Gin and tonic may be a British invention, but thanks to the constant influx of Brits to the Costa Brava, the Queen's favourite tipple has taken the Catalan capital by storm.

Barcelonans made it their own and call it 'gintonic', serving it in a balloon glass, with a sprig of rosemary, a slice of cucumber or even liquorice. The variations are limitless and customers are encouraged to handpick their gin and garnish, or leave it to the creative bartender. It is claimed Barcelonans are the biggest gin drinkers in the world per capita. A claim you will just have to verify for yourself.

The city's oldest coctelería, **Boadas Cocktail** (Carrer dels Tallers, 1; map F4) is the cocktail bar par excellence with polished wood and brass, zinc counters and leather bar stools. A merry hop away from La Rambla it was opened in 1933 by Havana-born Miguel Boadas. The top-shelf g&t served here mirrors the interior: authentic and classic.

At dark and sleek **Negroni** (Carrer de Joaquín Costa, 46; map E5), there is no menu, just let the barman quiz you on your tastes then wait to see what kind of g&t he concocts for you.

For a truly different g&t experience, head to **Ultramarinos Bar Casa Victor** (Carrer de Sant Pau, 126, tel 653 582424; map D2) for zingy and spicy orange, strawberry and cardamom, or a dessert-like apple and cinnamon gin cocktail while listening to wonderful piano music. This gin emporium counts no less than 80 brands from around the world and there are 25 different g&t styles to choose from. Hendricks aficionados flock to this cosy and colourful place whose cluttered bar is a true mixologist's laboratory. Try your luck with one of the wild daily specials such as a Hendricks with *pepino y pimienta rosa* (cucumber and pink pepper).

In the same street is **Ambar** (Carrer de Sant Pau, 77; map D2), a mellow-lit boudoir with walls hung with gilded mirrors, portraits, paintings and paraphernalia. Sit back and sip a classical g&t on one of the threadbare sofas under a vintage lamp, and gaze into an empty picture frame or sunglass lampshade.

Cassette (Caller de l'Est, 11; map E2) is the place to go to mix your ginger or lime gin and tonic with tapas, and indie or experimental music. A quirky mix matched by a quirky interior featuring retro televisions and music players, lamps covered with old cassettes, and shelves dotted with cult plastic collectables.

Don't be fooled by its name: **Bar Pesca Salada** (Carrer de la Cera,

32, tel 686 265309; map C3) may be a former fish shop and has kept the fish-theme going with a fish-scale ceiling but it is all about the gin now. The g&t's here are state-of-the-art and include the cult-classic cucumber, ginger, and tangerine.

And finally to the cheekily-named **Betty Ford's** (Carrer de Joaquín Costa, 56; map E5) a 1950s-style bar with wooden bistro chairs, old stone and glass features, and burgers to go with your cocktails. The humour is on show with the restaurant motto 'We all go a little mad now and then' wrapped around a large kitchen knife. This fun, charming, trendy little gem may will get you addicted...

Challenge your perceptions in a Baroque Rococo palace

From La Rambla the beautiful grand arcade of the **Palau de la Virreina** leads onto a series of cobblestoned courtyards, sweeping stairways and old coaching courts.

This magnificent 18th-century palace, adorned with both Baroque and Rococo decorative styles, was commissioned by Manuel Amat Junyent, the ostentatious viceroy of Peru, as a showcase for his wealth. Unfortunately for him, he died two years after it was completed in 1775, leaving his young wife to enjoy the palace, which became known as the palace of the 'Virreina' or vicereine.

The palace is home to the Institut de Cultura de l'Ajuntament de Barcelona, the Barcelona Town Hall's Culture Institute and LA VIRREINA **Centre de la Imatge**, an outward-looking contemporary arts and cultural centre whose major temporary exhibitions explore the image graphically and profoundly through art, photography, video installations, video art and literature.

There is also an information and ticket sales office for a wide range of cultural shows on the ground floor.

Palau de la Virreina; La Rambla, 99; tel: 933 161 000; Tue–Sun 12–8pm; free; map F3

Take a gastronomic acid trip at psychedelic Opera Samfaina

Located underneath the iconic Liceu theatre (see page 58), **Opera Samfaina** is the latest culinary venture of brothers Joan, Josep and Jordi Roca of El Celler de Can Roca fame, winner of three Michelin stars and best restaurant in the world accolade several times.

As you walk down the stairs through the red velvet curtains, it feels like you've eaten a magic mushroom and entered a phantasmagorical food emporium. As the animated theatre sets usher you in, your eyes are drawn to the video projections on the walls featuring Sant Jordí, patron saint of Catalonia, and his modern-day incarnation, chef Jordi Roca, who vanquishes Hercules to seal Barcelona's epicurean calling. On the way to your table you'll encounter a singing cow and a sausage-spouting dragon but the theatricals don't end there ... in fact they've only just begun.

This is an opera in four acts: with a *vermutería* bar, Odissea, La Diva and Marcat dining spaces all vying for your attention. Once seated at a circular table, with your own personal culinary croupier dishing up tapas-sized courses of the best Catalan produce, a riot of technicoloured sheep, cows, cheeses and vegetables zoom before you – even an angry Zeus pops up at your table. All this to the backdrop of a soundtrack performed by the orchestra of the Liceu opera house above.

This Catalan odyssey is the creation of visual artist Franc Aleu while the Roca brothers concocted the regional menu. The interactive dining experience promises to be a 'multisensorial gastronomic experience' fusing opera, art and food. A hotchpotch to match the restaurant's name, which means ratatouille.

Opera Samfaina; La Rambla, 51; tel: 934 817 871; www.operasamfaina.com; Mon-Sun 1pm–1am, Fri-Sat until 2am; map E2

Dodge dungeons and dragons at the Palau Güell

Just off La Rambla on a small side street is **Palau Güell**, built by Antoni Gaudí between 1885 and 1889 as the home of his patron, industrialist and politician Eusebi Güell – until he moved to his Park Güell residence (see page 143).

This petite urban palace looks like a multi-tiered jewellery box, packed with dazzling decorative details in wrought iron, pottery, glass, stone and wood. Spiralling up from a dungeon-like basement, once the stables, with a low vaulted ceiling of alternating patterned and coloured brick, it rises through lavishly hand-crafted interiors in the dining room and bedrooms and a grand central hall supported by a parabolic dome and arches. En route you will pass through an astounding intricate lab-yrinth of nooks and crannies com-posed of vestibules, antechamber and secret staircases decked with ceramic tiles, corbels and gargoyles. The crowning glory – as with most of Gaudí's works – is the rooftop, with its multicoloured mosaic chimneys overlooking the Rambla.

Güell's wanted his home to be peculiar and with the use of Moor-ish symbols, Gothic-style tracery and medieval winged beasts Gaudí certainly met the brief.

This Unesco treasure is part of the Starwood hotel chain's Unlock Art programme so access is free if you are staying at the nearby **Le Méridien** hotel in one of its Gaudí-inspired suites.

Palau Güell; Nou de la Rambla, 3–5; tel: 934 725 775; www.palauguell.cat; Apr–Oct 10am–8pm, Nov–Mar 10am–5.30pm; allocated visiting times as limited space inside; map E2
Le Méridien; La Rambla 111; tel: 93 318 6200; www.lemeridienbarcelona.com; map F4

Meet a giant smiling cat on Barcelona's newest Rambla

Though Barcelona's master planner Ildefons Cerdà ruminated a makeover of the old Chinatown *barri xino* in the early 1900s, it took nearly a century for the idea to materialise. This rundown working-class area in the southern part of El Raval closest to the port was transformed in 1995 with the addition of a major new artery of landscaped promenades.

Intersecting all the tiny cross streets, the **Rambla del Raval** starts at **Sant Pau del Camp** (Carrer Sant Pau, 101) church, whose 12th–14th century ensemble of courtyards and ethereal cloisters was built around a former 10th-century Romanesque monastery.

At the end of the 300m (985ft) palm-fringed avenue is Barcelona's answer to the Cheshire Cat, **El Gato del Botero** (map D2), by Colombian sculptor Fernando Botero. The lovable bronze fat cat looks on nonchalantly with a glib smile on his face.

For a sweet fix make a beeline to the **Pastelería La Estrella** (map E2) (Carrer Nou de la Rambla, 32), with its chocolate box facade of etched glass and engraved stone. This long-established pastry and sweet shop is replete with traditional homemade patisseries, including some vegan ones. You'll have to fight to get a seat at one of only two tables here. Best to take away and head to the **Filmoteca de Catalunya** (Plaça de Salvador Seguí, 1–9; map D2), a government-funded film archive which has daily screenings of classics and lesser-known films, exhibitions and an in-house bar.

Touch and feel your way through Barcelona's temple of contemporary art

The white-and-glass modernist structure of the **Museu d'Art Contemporani de Barcelona, MACBA**, dominates the Plaça dels Àngels.

Designed by US architect Richard Meier, a Le Corbusier disciple, the building is dazzling against the Mediterranean sky and gigantic in the context of the humble buildings beyond. The social and urban significance of the architecture in this once declining area has been as much of a talking point as the collection inside, which comprises Catalan, Spanish and some international art, mostly from the 20th century.

Defying pigeonholing as a museum, addressing multiple publics, presenting anti-exhibitions and confronting myths are all part of MACBA's manifesto.

In a space flooded with natural light, the ground-floor exhibitions blend documentaries with graphics, audio-visual projections, social commentary and philosophical probing. Others look at urbanism, the relationship between politics and culture, fiery debates on Barcelona planning and uncomfortable truths of the Civil War through images, archival photos and periodicals.

There are black and white beanbags for contemplation and headphones to get the most out of the exhibits. But don't expect it to be quiet. All the rooms open onto each other in a massive urban laboratory, a multimedia hands-on space, unorthodox, brazen and explicit.

Covered with louvered skylights, the loft like areas on successive levels house the Colleció MACBA and temporary exhibitions, looking for example at the links between art and sensory perception or experimentation with the physical and natural world.

Expect to be asked to do some strange things. Such as pop sweet and salty ice cubes in your mouth and walk through a massive ventilated installation as they melt. There is definite kids appeal here and they will also like the shop with its Barcelona colouring books, map poster books, monster-decorated lunch boxes made from recycled bottle bags, and voice-warping mini-recorders.

The spectacle continues outside. MACBA's large forecourt has evolved into a world-class skate-boarding space and is also a venue for local fiestas, music festivals and dance events. The square is a fascinating melting pot of local residents and cosmopolitan visitors.

MACBA; Plaça dels Àngels, 1; tel: 93 481 33 51/93 481 79 28; Mon, Wed–Fri, 11am–7.30pm, Sat 10am–9pm, Sun 10am–3pm, Tue closed; www.macba.cat; map E5

End a night at the opera with a Darth Vader ice cream

Launch pad for names such as Josep Carreras and Montserrat Caballé, the plush **Gran Teatre del Liceu** is as exquisite as the operas it plays host to.

The Renaissance-style lobby sets the tone with diagonal chequered black and white floor tiles, lavish candelabras, Doric gilded columns and an arched ceiling with inlaid panels of varying antique greens and mint hues. Then it's up the marble staircase with its majestic burgundy runner and gold standing candelabras.

The opera house has survived brawls between Verdi and Wagner supporters and two major fires since it opened its doors in 1847. The theatre season now covers a wide range of productions, from classical to ambitious avant-garde opera, ballet and recitals.

If you don't catch a performance you can still visit the Liceu on a guided tour taking in the lobby, the red-velvet and gilded auditorium (a replica of the original by architect Miquel Garriga i Roca, rebuilt after fire damage), and the Mirror Hall – once a favourite hobnobbing spot for Catalan aristocrats.

In keeping with the extravaganza of the Liceu is nearby ice-cream parlour **Rocambolesc Gelateria**, another part of the weird and wonderful Roca brothers culinary empire (see page 53). As its name suggests be prepared for some unusual but delicious frozen treats, and the Darth Vader and nose-shaped lollies make for the perfect selfie accessory.

Gran Teatro del Liceu; La Rambla 51–59; tel: 93 485 99 00; see website for tours timetable www.liceubarcelona.cat; map F2
Rocambolesc; La Rambla, 51; daily noon–11pm/midnight; map F2

Expand your mind in a culture laboratory

El Raval does love an acronym and rubbing shoulders with the MACBA, is the **Centre de Cultura Contemporània de Barcelona**, or CCCB.

The complex – a remodelling of the old almshouse Casa de la Caritat by architects Piñón and Viaplana – rivals MACBA for its architectural interest, the old white stone facade and courtyard of the almshouse contrasting wonderfully with the tilting glass and steel addition.

This brilliant contemporary arts centre offers a stimulating programme of cultural activities including music, dance, film, video, philosophy and seminars focusing on urban issues and the city as a social and cultural catalyst.

Acting like a big laboratory of urban and experimental ideas, the various spaces here include the CCCB Lab, host to international debates and probing discussions on the digital era, and literature platform Kosmopolis. The centre also organises the Xcèntric experimental film festival, a European Prize for Urban Public Space, and a Cultural Innovation International Prize.

In its bookshop you will find English-language books on art and culture, fashion, film and photography as well as a selection of nifty gifts.

Centre de Cultura Contemporània de Barcelona, CCCB; www.cccb.org; Tue–Sun, 11am–8pm; map E5

LA RIBERA AND EL BORN

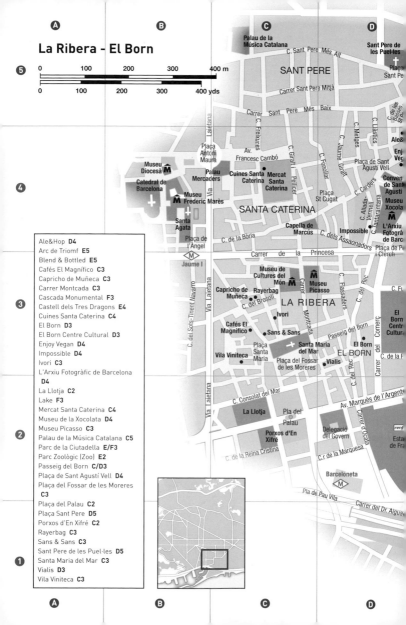

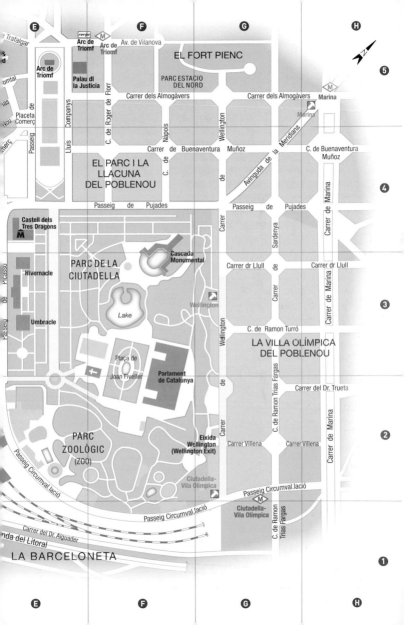

Shop 'til you drop in El Born, a trading hub since medieval times

It seems only natural that the El Born district, the hub of trade and commerce in medieval times, should today be home to a thriving boutique scene.

Many of the streets here are named after trades, a throwback to the medieval boom when guilds were formed to look after the interests of craftsmen. Wander down the narrow alleys past the guildhalls of the silversmiths on Carrer de l'Argenteria, the sword-makers on Carrer de l'Espaseria, the milliners on Carrer dels Sombrerers, the bonnet makers on Carrer de les Caputxes, and the leather tanners and bleachers on Carrer de la Blanqueria. Dozens of street names evoke the once prosperous textile industry, some focusing on very specific activities like Carrer dels Abaixadors, or street of the cloth-shearers, named after the craftsmen who clipped the fuzzy yarn off dried woollen fabric with large shearing scissors as part of the process of making cloth from wool.

Along the way you'll encounter shops reminiscent of past trades, such as tea emporium **Sans & Sans** (Carrer de l'Argenteria, 59; map C3) and its coffee sister shop **Cafés El Magnífico** (Carrer de l'Argenteria, 64; map C3), selling single-origin coffees since 1919, and **Vila Viniteca** (Carrer Agullers, 9; map C3), one of Spain's leading wine distributors.

Small ateliers here carve out a niche trade among a textile-loving population; some are ephemeral pop-ups tucked in hidden backstreets. At **Ivori** (Carrer del Mirallers, 7; map C3), find hand-crafted shawls, scarves, dresses and bags in a variety of colours and textures as well as espadrilles, jewellery and accessories all 'Made in Barcelona' by a collective of young Catalan designers.

There are other similar hole-in-the-wall studios and small clothing shops along Carrer del Brosolí. **Estudi Tèxtil La Barcalena** (1) sells handcrafted rugs and clothes made in natural fabrics in its no-frills surroundings. **Capricho de Muñeca** (1; map C3) is a rustic leather-making atelier, its bags and belts suspended between wooden rafters and worn stone floors. **Rayerbag** (4; map C3) is known for its handmade, colourful patchwork felt, leather and wool totes.

Far more established, **Vialis** (Carrer de la Vidrieria, 15; map D3) was actually born in El Born but now sells its Spanish-made

shoes in several outlets through out the city.

The commercial heyday of El Born ended with the fall of Mediterranean trade in the 16th century, but picked up again with the opening of the market on the Plaça Comercial in 1876. It now houses the **El Born Centre de Cultura** (see page 75), but the old market alcoves and dignified square are still a lively reminder of its glorious past.

Tree-lined Passeig del Born (map C/D3) leading off the square is an animated evening haunt. Stop for refreshment at **El Born** (26; map D3) a charming authentic bar with British racing green shutters, black and white diagonal tile floors, stained-glass windows and dark wooden bar stools.

Arty and neighbourly with tall colourful houses and a children's playground in the centre, the long, pedestrianised Carrer de l'Allada Vermell sports small boutiques and craft markets, café terraces and bars. Nearby, trendy **Impossible** (Caller Tantarantana 16; map D4) sells Polaroid cameras, other vintage paraphernalia and photophile trinkets laid out on mid-century modern furniture among art photos. Fittingly only a few steps away is the city's photography archive, **L'Arxiu Fotogràfic de Barcelona** (Plaça del Pons i Clech, 2; map D4), which puts on sporadic expos.

Indulge your inner chocoholic at the Museu de la Xocolata

Housed in a lovely burnt apricot-coloured ancient monastery, the **Museu de la Xocolata** taps into the city's love affair with chocolate, and there is no sweeter attraction in Barcelona for the kids.

Run by the Barcelona Provincial Confectionery Guild, the small museum displays exquisitely crafted and delectable chocolate sculptures such as replicas of La Sagrada Família and Disney icons. Pretty much everything here is edible, starting with your entrance ticket.

The museums retraces the long history of chocolate-making in Spain with a variety of parapher-nalia and short films. The city's deep-rooted chocolate infatuation truly began in the 16th century when conquistador Hernán Cortés brought back cocoa beans from the Aztecs in Mexico. Barcelona became an important gateway for chocolatiers all over Europe with shiploads of cocoa bean imports unloaded in its port. In the 18th century, under the chocolate-mad Bourbon rulers, Spain's military officers were given chocolate for breakfast and their personal guards were known as the *choco-lateros* because of the amount of chocolate they consumed.

Today, the chocolate tradition lives on thanks to Barcelona's inventive pastry makers and choc-olatiers – and the museum. Sign up to one of the classes from the menu of *Xocoexperiences*. You can learn how to paint with chocolate, create moulds or become a maître chocolatier for the day. The best way to end a visit here is to taste the heavenly stuff for yourself at either the shop or the café.

Museu de la Xocolata; Carrer Comerç, 36; tel; 93 268 78 78; Mon–Sat 10am–7pm, until 8pm 15 June–15 Sept, until 3pm Sun; guided tours available; www.museuxocolata.cat; map D4

Awaken your senses at a Modernista concert hall extravaganza

The Unesco-listed **Palau de la Música Catalana** is a sumptuous concert hall designed by leading Modernista architect Lluís Domènech i Montaner in 1908.

The facade is crowded with sculptures and dazzling mosaics reflecting the Catalan musical tradition. But the real spectacle is inside: a jaw-dropping profusion of ornate carvings, flower and fruit motifs, ironwork, sculptures and stained glass. It is the only concert hall in Europe to be naturally lit, through its huge teardrop skylight decorated in magnificent stained glass.

Oscar Tusquets' 2008 extension, featuring organic motifs in keeping with the Modernista original, houses the Petit Palau, a concert hall for chamber music as well as an elegant restaurant.

One of the best ways to visit this Modernista gem is to take a guided tour. They are popular, so it is worth booking in advance. Alternatively, pop in for a coffee or tapas in its foyer bar to sample the atmosphere and see plenty of Modernista detail – or, even better, attend one of the concerts in its busy classical season. The Palau is the home of the Orfeó Català, the Catalan Choral Society, so you could also try and catch one of their recitals.

Carrer del Palau de la Música, 4–6; tel: 93 295 72 00; www.palaumusica.cat; map C5

Take to the water in Barcelona's green oasis, the venerable Parc de la Ciutadella

Barcelona's oldest and most visited park, the **Parc de la Ciutadella** is home to a delightful mix of gardens, fountains, statues, a **lake** (map F3), waterfall, rotunda, bandstands, children's playgrounds, cafés, a zoo, a colony of grey herons, a geology museum and even the Catalan Parliament.

Built on the former Bourbon citadel (hence its name) erected to control the renegade city, in 1868 General Prim ceded the land over to Barcelona for conversion into a public park. He has a statue in the park. A much needed green space in the rapidly industrialising and crowded city. 'Gardens in cities serve the same purpose as lungs in the human body', declared the park's architect Josep Fontseré, they 'allow breathing'.

Inaugurated in 1872, it was tweaked for the 1888 Universal Exhibition, and graced with the enormous red-brick **Arc de Triomf** (map E5) that serves as a grand entranceway today. Fontserè's young assistant, Antoni Gaudí, had a hand in its design, and is credited with much of the rocky carvings and some of the decorative motifs.

The park enjoys a great location near the port and with a backdrop of coastal mountains. It provides a fantastic leisure area for all generations. Its planted promenades and squares parade an exotic assortment of plants and trees: ferns and foxgloves, palms, poplar and plane trees, lime and nettle trees, French oleanders, date palms and endangered species such as the Gingko, or maidenhair tree. There's also the large **Arbre de la Memoria** – from the suitably named species *Bellaombra* given its canopy provides shade for many. A semi-evergreen originating from South America and somewhat resembling a fig tree, it is a tribute to breast cancer sufferers.

This is a real city park, full of skateboards and footballs, prams and toddlers. There are bicycles made for six to hire, as well as rowing boats on the pretty lake (you can rent one by the half hour for up to five people). Nearby, kids love climbing the trunk of the giant mammoth stone sculpture.

It is easy to while away half a day here. Join the dozens of picnickers unwinding on the lawns, or continue along among the perfectly trimmed hedges of Japanese mock orange shrub to the much-photographed **Cascada Monumental** (map F3), a Roman-style tiered fountain featuring a sculpture of Eros and winged dragons.

Children will enjoy a visit to the **Barcelona Zoo** (map E2) which takes up half of the park; its dolphin show is a big draw. Or you could explore the geology and palaeontology collections of the **Laboratori de Natura** located within the **Castell dels Tres Dragons** (map E4), a Modernista folly designed by architect Lluís Domènech i Montaner in 1888 as the café-restaurant for the World Fair.

Parc de la Ciutadella; map E/F3

Follow in the footsteps of a young Picasso

Pablo Picasso spent his formative years in Barcelona, studying at the Reial Acadèmia Catalana de Belles Arts de Sant Jordi, an art school housed in the upper floors of the Casa Llotja de Mar on Pla del Palau.

Commonly called **La Llotja** (Passeig d'Isabel II; map C2), this Gothic building has retained its medieval interior, inludign its magnificent Gothic hall, but its facade was added centuries later in the neoclassical style. Stroll into its old orange-tree courtyard, full of neoclassical marble sculptures. The building is still home to the School of Fine Arts and the Barcelona Stock Exchange Library. Picasso's father, a painter himself, also taught here.

Opposite La Llotja was Picasso's home, in the long porticoed building known as **Porxos d'En Xifré** (map C2). The Ruíz-Picasso family set up house here when they came to live in Barcelona. Nudging Port Vell, it was built in 1840 by Josep Xifré i Casas, the wealthiest property tycoon of the time who made his fortune in the sugar plantations of Cuba.

Picasso enjoyed going up to the rooftop, where he painted some of his first city landscapes, capturing the roofs, the sea and the Mediterranean light. Many of them are on show at the Picasso Museum (see page 74).

Gaudí lampposts

In Pla del Palau, look out for the bold, allegorical and almost lifelike street lamps. These cast-iron structures with a marble base and polychrome features are the work of one Antoni Gaudí and come with either three or six branches. The three-branched ones are adorned with the shield of Barcelona with inverted crowns on top and on the six-branched ones there is a snake with a winged caduceus, representing Mercury the God of Commerce – fitting as La Llotja was once the city's stock exchange.

Soak in the relaxed, bohemian atmosphere of Sant Pere

The narrow cobblestoned and largely car-free streets of **Sant Pere** confer the area a distinct laid-back feel and village atmosphere.

A micro barrio within the Sant Pere–Santa Caterina neighbourhood, village life here hinges on the gently sloped streets around the **Plaça de Sant Pere** (map D5) through to **Plaça de Sant Augustí Vell** (map D4). Strolling away, you will stumble upon little squares with community vegetable gardens planted among park benches and picnic tables, laundry cascading from tiered balconies Naples-style, and children on scooters and bikes or playing ball games.

There are Romanesque treasures to watch out for too, such as the pretty 10th-century church of **Sant Pere de les Puelles** (Carrer de Lluís el Piadós, 1; map D5). This former Benedictine convent survived Arab sieges, fires and the expulsion of its community of nuns in the 19th century.

Residents of Sant Pere include young families, artists, artisans and designers, all attracted to the bohemian character of the barrio. And there are plenty of quirky shops and bars for them to eat and quench their thirst.

One of them is the narrow **Ale&Hop** (Carrer de les Basses de Sant Pere, 10; map D4), where craft beers and vegetarian food are served up at a gleaming corrugated tin bar.

Equally tiny but cosy, **Enjoy Vegan**'s (Plaça de Sant Augustí Vell, 10; map D4) tasty fare includes aubergine and carrot empanadas.

At **Blend & Bottled** (Passatge de l'Hort dels Velluters, 5; map E5) there are two-hour wine tasting sessions accompanied by cheese and charcuterie platters all served up on communal tables.

To eat in one of Sant Pere's landmarks, head to the **Mercat de Santa Caterina** (Avinguda de Francesc Cambó, 16; map C4) for some tapas at Cuines Santa Caterina restaurant under the market's wonderful mosaic-tiled undulating roof.

Mercat de Santa Caterina; Mon 7.30am–2pm, Tue, Wed & Sat 7.30am–3.30pm, Thu–Fri 7.30am-8.30pm; map C4

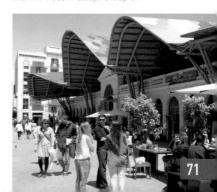

Bask in Gothic splendour then pay your respects to Catalan patriots at Santa Maria del Mar

Considered by many – and justly so – to be the city's most beautiful church, **Santa Maria del Mar** was built in the 14th century on the site of a Roman amphitheatre in the lower part of the Ribera, right there where the city meets the sea, hence its name Santa Maria 'of the sea'. The Virgin Mary is also the patroness of mariners and 'Star of the Sea', the epitaph traditionally assigned to her.

The church was built relatively quickly, in just 55 years, resulting in a purity of style which ranks it as the most perfect example of Gothic church architecture in Catalonia. Nicknamed 'cathedral of La Ribera', it was considered the people's church as all the local corporations collaborated in the building, and it became a symbol of the economic and political power of Catalonia during that period.

Plaça del Fossar de les Moreres

Adjacent to Santa Maria del Mar is Plaça del Fossar de les Moreres, a memorial to the fallen in the 1714 siege of Barcelona, who are buried here in the former cemetery.

In 1989, the architect Carme Fiol revamped the square laying the ground with 'brick as red as the blood that had been spilt'. Later came Alfons Viaplana's equally sanguine monument, with its eternal flame burning on top.

In the shade of the mulberry trees which give the square its name, a plaque reads: 'In the graveyard of the mulberry trees no traitor shall be buried; even if our flags are lost, it will be the urn of honour.' The poem by 19th-century Catalan playwright Serafí Pitarra is read out every year on 11 September to mark Catalonia's National Day, La Diada.

The church's architectural purity and elegant unadorned style is visible inside and out. Arranged around three naves, the cavernous interior is filled with light despite its solid appearance. The octagonal columns are 13m (43ft) apart, a distance no other medieval structure was able to achieve.

Join in one of the guided tours to learn about the history of the neighbourhood and the impact the 15th-century earthquake had on the church's facade, rose window and vaults. It'll take you up and down from the crypt all the way up to the rooftop to enjoy a sweeping view over medieval La Ribera.

Santa Maria del Mar; Plaça de Santa Maria, 1; Mon–Sat 9am–1.30pm & 4.30–8pm, Sun from 10.30am. Tours in English May–Oct, Mon–Sun at 2 & 3pm; map C3

Palace-hop to the Picasso Museum in one of medieval Barcelona's poshest streets

La Ribera's **Carrer Montcada** (map C3) might only be small and narrow but it's packed with lavish Gothic palaces, all set around a central courtyard and monumental staircase, and beautified over time with Renaissance, Baroque and neoclassical frills.

Named after the members of the noble Montcada family who died during the conquest of Mallorca (1229), it linked the waterfront with the commercial areas, when Catalonia's overseas trading was at its height. The merchants' palaces reflect this former prosperity.

Today five of these palaces make up the **Museu Picasso**: Palau Aguilar, Palau Meca, Palau Baró de Castellet, Palau Finestres and Casa Mauri.

Arriving in Barcelona in 1895, aged 14, young Pablo spent nine years here before leaving for Paris, and was deeply influenced by the Catalan Modernista style.

The museum opened in 1963, at Picasso's request. It has the most complete collection of Picasso's early works, including sketches in school books and a masterly portrait of his mother, created when he was only 16 years old. The Blue Period (1901–04) is also well represented, with notably his *Rooftops of Barcelona*. Also on show are a series of ceramics.

It is an absorbing collection, although there are only a few of Picasso's later works, notably the fascinating studies of *Las Meninas* dating from the 1950s.

It'll be hard not to buy anything in the well-stocked shop and there is also a lovely courtyard café for that all-important post-visit refreshment.

Museu Picasso; Carrer de Montcada, 15–23; tel: 932 563 000; Tue–Sun, 9am–7pm, Thu 9am–9.30pm; www.museupicasso.bcn.cat; map C3

Gaze into the city below in a former art nouveau market

The magnificent wrought-iron **Mercat del Born**, designed by Catalan architect Antoni Rovira i Trias and built between 1874 and 1876 by master builder Josep Fontserè i Mestre and engineer Josep Maria Cornet i Mas, was the city's first covered market.

It closed down in 1971 but was saved from demolition in the mid-1990s. After years of indecision it was relaunched in 2013 as the **El Born Centre de Cultura i Memòria**. During its restoration in 2002, the ruins of houses demolished on the orders of the Bourbon monarchs in 1714 to make way for a citadel in the aftermath of the War of the Spanish Succession were unearthed. They are now on display as part of the *Ciutat del Born*, bringing that buried history back into the collective memory.

Impressive chunks of the houses remain, allowing researchers to determine not only how the residents lived but who they were, their trades and lifestyles. The exhibition 'Barcelona 1700' explains the history of the area in the 1700s as well as the siege.

Anyone can walk in off the street and peep into the dig, and the interiors of the old market. Children seem to get a particular kick from doing so and they can also participate in the CCM's cultural programme of puppet shows, art and dance, literature, music and film.

El Born Centre Cultural; Plaça Comercial, 12; tel: 932 566 850; Tue–Sun 10am–8pm; ticket required to visit the ruins up-close and the exhibition 'Barcelona 1700'.

BARCELONETA AND PORT VELL

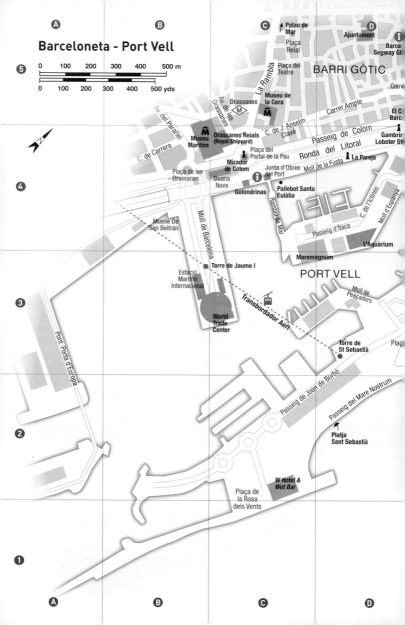

Barceloneta - Port Vell

A   **B**   **C**   **D**

5

0   100   200   300   400   500 m

0   100   200   300   400   500 yds

BARRI GÒTIC

Palau de Mar

Plaça Reial

Ajuntament

Barce Segway Gl

Plaça del Teatre

La Rambla

El C Barc

Carrer Ample

Museu de la Cera

Drassanes

Av. de les Drassanes

Passeig de Colom

Gambrir Lobster S

C. de J. Anselm Clavé

Museu Marítim

Drassanes Reials (Royal Shipyard)

C. de Carrera

Av. del Paral·lel

Ronda del Litoral

La Pareja

Plaça del Portal de la Pau

Mirador de Colom

Moll de la Fusta

Plaça de les Drassanes

Junta d'Obres del Port

Duana Nova

Pailebot Santa Eulàlia

Golondrinas

C. de l'itineo

Moll d'Espanya

4

Passeig d'Itaca

L'Aquàrium

Muelle De San Beltrán

Rambla de Mar

Maremàgnum

Moll de Barcelona

Torre de Jaume I

PORT VELL

Estació Marítim Internacional

Moll de Pescadors

3

Port Porta d'Europa

World Trade Center

Transbordador Aeri

Torre de St Sebastià

Plaç

Passeig de Joan de Borbó

Passeig del Mare Nostrum

2

Platja Sant Sebastià

W Hotel & Wet Bar

Plaça de la Rosa dels Vents

1

A   **B**   **C**   **D**

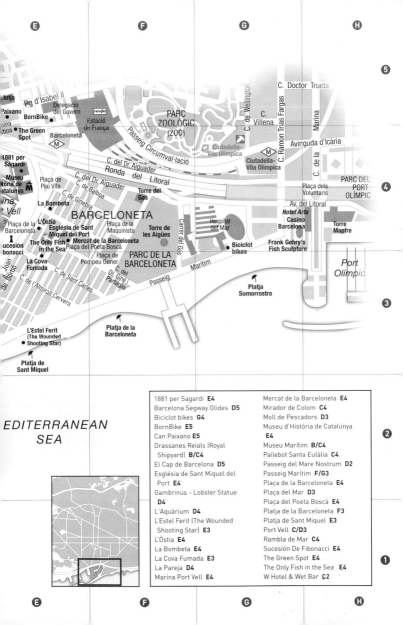

E   **F**   **G**   **H**

5

C. Doctor Trueta

Pg d'Isabel II
Delegacio
del Govern
renfe
PARC
ZOOLÒGIC
(ZOO)

C. de Wellington
C.
Villena
C. Ramon Trias Fargas
Marina

Paixano
BornBike
Estació
de França
Ciutadella
Vila Olímpica

**The Green
Spot**

Barceloneta
Ⓜ

Passeig Circumval·lació

Avinguda d'Icària

1881 per
Sagardi
C. del Dr. Aiguader
Ronda del Litoral
Ciutadella-
Vila Olímpica Ⓜ

C. de la

5

Museu
tòria de
atalunya Ⓜ
Plaça de
Pau Vila
C. de Balboa
Torre del
Gas

PARC DEL
PORT
OLÍMPIC

4

na Vell
La Bombeta
C. de Ginebra

BARCELONETA

Plaça dels
Voluntaris
Av. del Litoral

Plaça de la
Barceloneta
L'Òstia
Església de Sant
Miquel del Port
Plaça de la
Maquinista
Torre de
les Aigües
Hospital
del Mar
Hotel Arts
Casino
Barcelona
Torre
Mapfre

ucesión
bonacci
The Only Fish
in the Sea
Plaça del Poeta Boscà
Mercat de la Barceloneta
Plaça de
Pompeu Gener

Biciclot
bikes

La Cova
Fumada

PARC DE LA
BARCELONETA

Carrer del Gas

Frank Gehry's
Fish Sculpture

Port
Olímpic

C. de Sant Carles
C. del
Dr. Giné i
Partadés
Passeig
Marítim

3

C. de l'Almirall Cervera

Platja
Somorrostro

L'Estel Ferit
(The Wounded
● Shooting Star)

Platja de la
Barceloneta

Platja de
Sant Miquel

2

1

E   **F**   **G**   **H**

Take in a view and guess what Columbus is pointing to at the Mirador de Colom

Dominating the high seas and the Barcelona skyline from his lofty position near the harbour, Christopher Columbus's effigy tops off the 60m (197ft) high **Mirador de Colom**.

Commonly referred to as the Columbus Monument, the grandiose cast-iron Corinthian column rises up from the **Plaça del Portal de la Pau** at the foot of La Rambla.

Installed ahead of the 1888 Universal Exposition, the monument commemorates Cristòfor Colom, as he's known locally, on his visit to Barcelona in 1493 to report back from his voyage to America to King Ferdinand and Queen Isabella.

It has been called the Catalan answer to Nelson's Column in London's Trafalgar Square, right down to the lions at the base, for Catalan nationalists took Columbus to heart as their very own Vasco de Gama, raising him on a very big pedestal.

The Italian-born navigator was given a hero's welcome despite famously failing to reach the American mainland on his 1492 voyage, arriving in the Bahamas and Cuba instead. In fact the statue portrays the great explorer holding a navigational chart in his left hand and ostensibly pointing out the route to America with his right – though some claim he's actually pointing in the direction of Libya.

Take a lift up to the viewing gallery, whose views throw like a fish net over the harbour and La Rambla leading down to it.

Mirador de Colom; Plaça del Portal de la Pau; daily 8.30am–8.30pm; www.barcelonaturisme.com; map C4

Watch sharks swim over your head at the Aquarium

Children big and small will love a visit to **L'Aquàrium de Barcelona**. The highlight here is walking through the long glass tunnel as though on the seafloor, and getting up close and personal with sting-rays, moray eels, ocean sunfish, gilthead sea breams, and the stars of the show, tiger sharks and sand-bar sharks.

With over 8,000 different fish and other aquatic wonders, the colourful marine communities of the Mediterranean and the tropical seas are shown off in all their glory in gleaming tanks and basins, allowing you close obser-vation of their weird and wonderful behaviour. Informative panels are on hand and a number of smaller themed aquariums have interac-tive modules.

The children's zone Explora! is an interactive space of marine world pedagogy with 50 touchy-feely activities for discovering the natural world of three Mediterra-nean coastline environments: the marshes of the Ebro Delta, a corner of the Costa Brava and an underwa-ter cave in the Medes Islands.

Visitors can also get involved in the feeding of fish and watch penguins have their dinner. Special experiences to be booked in advance include diving with the sharks and children's slumber parties where they sleepover at the aquarium and see how the marine world wakes up.

L'Aquàrium de Barcelona; Moll d'Espanya del Port Vell; tel: 932 21 74 74; daily 10am–7.30/8pm; www.aquariumbcn.com; map D4

81

Feel the heat of a Barceloneta potato bomb

A fiery taste sensation and a culinary legend, Barcelona's *bombes de patate* – an explosive mixture of spicy potato, minced meat and hot sauce – are a tangy tapas tradition in the small restaurants of **Barceloneta**.

The tavern **La Cova Fumada**, tucked away in a small side street near the port, claims to be the birthplace of the delightful fluffy, fried potato croquettes. Josep Maria Solé is the third-generation owner of the family-run establishment where in 1955 his grandmother, Maria Pla, apparently invented the delicacies, still a house speciality and a closely guarded recipe. Here the faithful come in droves, sit at the bar or at the small marble and cast-iron tables, and down hearty dishes such as stewed *garbanzos* and salted cod, and *bombes* in force.

Another favourite for *bombes* fans is nearby **La Bombeta**, a cosy no-frills bar-restaurant with a rust-red painted facade and retro lighting, famed for its authentic tapas and atmosphere.

La Cova Fumada; Carrer del Baluard, 56;
tel 93 221 40 60; map E3
La Bombeta; Carrer de la Maquinista, 3;
tel 933 19 94 45; map E4

Delve into Barcelona's seafaring past in the world's largest and best-preserved medieval shipyard

Christopher Columbus must feel right at home standing as he is alongside the 14th-century medieval shipyard, the **Drassanes Reials** (map B/C4).

It was in the service of King Ferdinand and Queen Isabella of Spain that he sailed towards the Americas in 1492. And this Royal Shipyard was where the Catalan military and mercantile fleet was built. Erected in 1378, enclosed by the city's 15th-century outer wall and greatly enlarged in the 17th century, the massive Drassanes launched thousands of ships. At its height it was turning out 30 war galleys at a time. The shipyard is one of the best-preserved examples of Gothic civil architecture in the world.

Within the shipyard is the **Museu Marítim**, charting Catalonia's seafaring history with a fine collection of fishing boats and model ships, including a full-scale replica of the 16th-century galley, the *Reial*, in which Don Juan of Austria led the Christian fleet to defeat the Turks in the battle of Lepanto in 1571.

The museum organises a range of cultural activities, and the schooner on the quayside, *Santa Eulàlia*, can also be visited.

Museu Marítim; Avinguda de les Drassanes, s/n; tel: 93 342 9920; daily 10am–8pm; free Sun after 3pm; www.mmb.cat; map B/C4
Santa Eulàlia (tour in Spanish only) Tue– Sun 10am–8.30pm; no wheelchair access

Drink in the views from the rooftop terrace of the Palace of the Sea

The elegant arches of the **Palau de Mar**, a former warehouse complex, are unmissable as you amble around the harbour. In the heart of Port Vell on the crossroads of Barceloneta and the Gothic quarter, it was built in the 1890s as the headquarters of the Magatzems Generals de Comerç store. Although industrial in design, there are touches of Venice's Doge's Palace in its Gothic style window decoration and cornerstones.

The only old trading warehouse to survive the wholesale renovation of the port area, it was restored in 1992 and baptised the 'Palace of the Sea'.

Upstairs is the **Museu d'Història de Catalunya** with chronological displays on the region's history from prehistory to the present, including the cataclysmic Franco era and the 1702–15 War of Succession – all part of the permanent exhibition *Memòria d'un País*. There are a range of special activities for children and adults, the latter focusing on such topics as the imaginary presence of Don Quixote in Barcelona.

After your visit, head to the rooftop restaurant **1881 per Sagardi** for a light bite or long drink and extraordinary harbour views.

Museu Palau de Mar; Plaça Pau Vila, 3; tel: 93 225 4700; Tue–Sat 10am–7pm, Wed until 8pm; www.mhcat.cat; map E4
1881 per Sagardi; tel: 932 210 050; daily 10am–midnight, Fri–Sat until 1am

Walk, jog, bike or rollerblade along the Passeig Marítim

Unleash your sporty self on Barcelona's tremendous waterfront esplanade the **Passeig Marítim** (map F/G3), which meanders for 4.3km (2.6 miles) from the Parc de la Barceloneta to the Parc del Fòrum. The glistening seaside strip offers unlimited opportunities for filling your lungs with fresh salty air whatever your means of transport.

While the fleets of eye-catching red bikes of the public bike-sharing scheme *Bicing* are not up for grabs (they are for residents' use only), there are plenty of other places to rent a bike for a day or a week, or you can also join a bike tour.

The cluster of yellow bikes on the Passeig Marítim belong to **Biciclot** (33; map G4) and are available for hire from around €5 an hour or €17 for a day, helmet and lock included.

Further north at **BornBike** (Carrer de la Marquesa, 1; map E5), a fee of €15 a day includes a map and plenty of info on the best bike routes. Both companies offer a range of tours, including a tapas circuit, for those who want to mix exercise with pleasure. Tandem bikes are also available.

With 200km (125 miles) of cycling lanes and mostly flat terrain, Barcelona is bike-friendly, but here you can count on some sensational waterfront views.

Hang out at Barceloneta's beaches and seaside squares

You will want to linger on the **Plaça del Mar** for a while. This sculpture-filled beach square is a happening hub of beach life, buskers and outdoor activity opening onto a string of city beaches and the blue Mediterranean beyond.

It's an outdoor arena for musicians, posers, beach-goers and sporty souls. Join in on regular performances by solo musicians, singers and bands that turn the wide sweep of steps by the **Platja de Sant Miquel** (map E3) into a beachfront concert.

In the northern corner of the quadrangle, the grid of narrow streets are reminders of Barceloneta's maritime history, which lives on in the rowdy bars around the Carrers del Mar and dels Pescadors.

By the Platja de Sant Miquel, take a moment away from the hedonistic beach atmosphere to reflect on the Mediterranean's darker side: a rust-coloured tribute marked '2016, 5079' is a sobering reminder of the number of migrants who drowned in the Mediterranean in 2016. On the memorial, the city caretakers pledge 'to never cease the demand for a legal and safe passage to Europe and a change of course

in asylum policies', a strong indicator of Barcelona's fervent migrant policy.

Back on the **Passeig Marítim de la Barceloneta**, on the beach itself you can't miss a remarkable sculp-

ture by German artist Rebecca Horn, **L'Estel Ferit** (*The Wounded Shooting Star*; pictured page 76; map E3). The 10m (33ft) -high lopsided stack of four iron and glass cubes with windows is a nod to the faded but charming seafront restaurants, *xiringuitos*, which disappeared from the coastline during the pre-Olympics clean-up.

Plaça del Mar; map D3

Scout for street art in Port Vell

While some of the public artworks in Port Vell are highly conspicuous icons, others are virtually hidden or unknown gems. But all transform the waterfront to an open-air gallery for everyone to enjoy.

The most widely recognised is Roy Lichtenstein's red-and-white polka dot Pop Art wonder *El Cap de Barcelona* (Passeig de Colom, 32; map D5), standing 20m (65ft) high at one end of the port with its bold Mediterranean colours of blue, red and yellow mosaic tiles. The 'Head of Barcelona' depicts a woman looking out to sea, silhouetted against a bright blue Barcelona sky. Created for the 1992 Olympics, it was part of a series by the American artist called Brushstroke, and according to him an unequivocal Gaudiesque tribute.

During the port's 1990s revamp, many new works of art were installed. Directly opposite *El Cap*, on the portside promenade **Ronda Littoral**, is the appropriately maritime-themed giant lobster statue *Gambrinus* (map D4) by Spanish artist and graphic designer Javier Mariscal.

Among the more discrete sculptures are a series of copper figures of amorous couples, tucked between garden beds or blending into the stonework along the docks of Moll de Bosch i Alsina, popularly known as **Moll de la Fusta**.

One such work, *La Pareja* (*The Couple*; map D4) by Chilean artist Lautaro Díaz, shows a bronze couple seated on the edge of the port. Reminiscent of Giacometti's spindly forms, the mermaid- and merman-looking figures have no arms and their feet are glued together and fin-like.

Mathematical Art

Walking along the pedestrianised Paseo Juan de Borbón in Port Vell you will tread over a sequence of red neon letters recessed in glass encasings. The *Successió de Fibonacci* is a sequence of numbers, each the sum of the previous two: 0, 1, 1, 2, 3, 5, 8, 13, 21, 34, etc., created by Italian contemporary artist Mario Merz in 1992.

Get romantic with a night-time stroll on the waterfront

The city's most historic port has a magical atmosphere at night, with the play between moonlight and the swirly neon-lit footbridges.

So put on some comfortable espadrilles and stroll hand-in-hand along its coves and docks stretching about 1.8km (1.2 miles) – a breezy 30-minute walk – from Barceloneta to the Columbus Monument.

Once an obsolete harbour, **Port Vell** (map C/D3) was resuscitated during the massive urban renewal project prior to the 1992 Olympics. Start at the **Moll dels Pescador** (Fishermen's Wharf; map D3), brimming with maritime character and echoing sea shanties of times past, the sound of bobbing boats and their reflections on the water only adding to the charm. Continue around the masts and marinas past the **Marina Port Vell** (map E4) and its new luxury superyacht hub OneOcean Vell.

The wide portside promenade stretching between the wharf and the Passeig de Colom is dotted with flowerbeds, palms and statues. Then it's on to the undulating wooden walkway, the **Rambla de Mar** (map C4), a sculpture in itself. Designed in 1994 by the architect duo Albert Viaplana and Helio Piñón, the minimalist structure is

supported over the water by two iron arms which open every hour on the dot to allow recreational boats through.

Back on the harbour walk, admire the historic three-masted schooner, *Pailebot Santa Eulàlia* (map C4). Built in 1918 and named after Barcelona's co-patron saint, it is docked at **Moll de Bosch i Alsina** when not out at sea.

Soak up the old maritime airs of the village of Barceloneta

In a stark contrast to the new marina area, Barceloneta – once the home of the city's fishing community – retains its historic charm and sense of neighbourhood.

This is especially true in the peninsula's interior. Just a hop skip and jump away from the Platja Sant Miquel beach, the peaceful back-street squares and markets move at a different pace. Along sinewy cobblestoned streets, old-time bars still bear their *licorería* liquor store signs, and maritime-themed boutiques sport wooden rope signs.

One hundred percent sea-centric with its scalloped roe-hued exterior strung with fishnets is **The Only Fish**

in the Sea (Carrer de l'Atlàntida, 47; map E4), selling local and imported jewellery, artwork and linen.

The main cobblestoned square **Plaça de la Barceloneta** (map F3) was at the heart of the old fishing village. The only open space within a grid of closely spaced streets here you will find shops, cafés and eateries in quaint tall houses with miniature balconies.

Overlooking the barrio is the 1755 Baroque **Església de Sant Miquel del Port** (Carrer Sant Miquel, 39; map E4), with its distinctive brawny sculpture of the archangel Michael wielding a sword and chain above the main door. Inside are wall inscriptions in latin all dedicated to the protector saint. For a century the church had no bell tower, just a mini cupola, due to strict orders to keep Barceloneta sufficiently low to fire cannons from the nearby Parc de la Ciutadella overhead, in order to deter the rebellious Catalans.

For some tapas or *calamars* head to the fresco-walled taverna, **L'Òstia** (Plaça de la Barceloneta, 1; map E4). Beyond the dungeon-like window grills are bright modern interiors.

On the adjacent square, **Plaça del Poeta Boscà** (map E4), the historic **Mercat de la Barceloneta** occupies a Modernista-style industrial wrought-iron structure. Initially an outdoor market frequented by sailors and fishermen, the undercover market built in 1884 by Antoni Rovira i Trias also of Mercat de Sant Antoni fame (see page 120) received the designer treatment in the late 2000s.

Architect Josep Miàs, a contemporary and colleague of Enric Miralles – creator of the Parc Diagonal Mar (see page 101) – set out to preserve the original metallic structure yet incorporate modern elements and infrastructure. Exercising a strong eco-responsibility, this was the city's first market to integrate photovoltaic solar panels, which now generate 40 percent of its total energy consumption, and it has also received accolades for its waste management project.

The solar panel setup acts as a rooftop to the café terraces spreading out over the square. Inside, shop for vegetables and cheese, olives and olive oil or sit down at one of its seafood restaurants.

Mercat de la Barceloneta; Plaça de la Poeta Boscà, 1; Mon–Thu 7am–2pm, Fri 7am–8pm, Sat 7am–3pm; map E4

Have a rowdy glass of cava then retreat to a vegetarian haven all in the same street

Sit yourself at the bar of **Can Paixano (La Xampanyeria)** – or more realistically stand shoulder to shoulder – and enjoy a glass of sparkling cava with locals. Ham and industrial design lamps hang from the wooden rafters in this buzzing, characterful delicatessen-cum-cava cellar founded in 1969. You could try the ultra-tasty sandwiches and various tapas here or save yourself for our next stop.

Only a few steps away but miles away in terms of ambience, is **The Green Spot**, whose ship galley appearance is in keeping with its proximity to Port Vell. A long oak panelled corridor leads to the dining area, which exudes monastic peace with its celestial cross-vault ceiling of low white-stone arches, soft lighting and interior garden.

The Green Spot aims to please and their motto 'veggie for veggies, veggie for non veggies' sums up the wide appeal of the vegetarian and vegan creations here. The tasty fare includes spinach and chard or black bean burger with pretzel bread, various macrobiotic options, Japanese seaweed salad with Umeboshi sesame vinaigrette, or you can just go for a simple dish of wild greens with peas and avocado. The veggie burgers are served with colourful dips resembling pots of pastel paint. They all marry perfectly well with a glass of organic DO Garnacha, a *denominación de origen* Grenache from the Penedès wine-growing region southwest of the city. Then dessert on carrot cake with a cashew and vanilla frosting or a refreshing lemon and celery sorbet.

And as you could expect from such a trendy place, there is live music Tuesday and Thursday evenings.

Can Paixano; Carrer de la Reina Cristina, 7; tel: 933 100 839; www.canpaixano.com
The Green Spot; Carrer de la Reina Cristina, 12; tel: 938 02 55 65;
www.encompaniadelobos.com
All map E4

Get fit with the beautiful people of W Barcelona at a beach boot camp

Commanding the most sensational waterfront location, the **W Barcelona** hotel rises up like a giant silvery glass sail at the end of the Barceloneta boardwalk, and locals now refer to it naturally as *La Vela* (the sail).

Designed by Ricardo Bofill in 2010, the 26-storey architectural landmark stands at Nova Bocana, the new entry to Barcelona's port reclaimed from the sea.

Fabulous from top to bottom: its **Eclipse** rooftop bar offers stupendous city and sea views and at ground level, the **Wet Bar**'s large terrace and infinity pool spill into the Mediterranean. The palm-fringed area filled with sun loungers is a major venue for pool partying, cocktails, snacks and DJ house beats day and night from April to October.

Stretching either side of the hotel, the beachfront strip of the **Passeig del Mare Nostrum** (map D2) is a fitness fanatic's paradise. Join flotillas of morning joggers here continuing along the **Passeig Marítim** or happen upon one of **Beach Fit**'s early morning or evening boot-camp style workouts held on the **Platja de la Barceloneta** (meeting on the Plaça Del Mar outside the restau-

rant Buenas Migas; www.beach fitbcn.com; map F3).

W Barcelona; Plaça de la Rosa dels Vents, 1; tel: 93 295 28 00; www.w-barcelona. com; map C2

VILA OLÍMPICA
AND EL POBLENOU

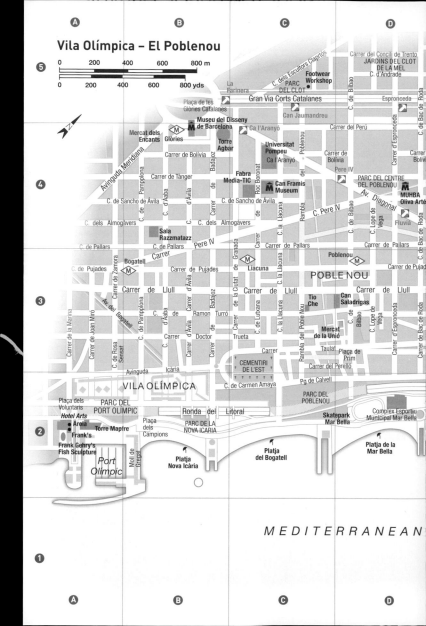

Vila Olímpica – El Poblenou

0 200 400 600 800 m
0 200 400 600 800 yds

JARDINS DEL CLOT DE LA MEL

Carrer del Concili de Trento
C. d'Andrade
Espronceda

La Farinera

C. dels Escultors Claprtos

Footwear Workshop
PARC DEL CLOT

Gran Via Corts Catalanes

Plaça de les Glòries Catalanes

Can Jaumandreu

Museu del Disseny de Barcelona

Ca l'Aranyó

Carrer del Perú

Mercat dels Encants
Glòries
Torre Agbar

Universitat Pompeu Fabra
Ca l'Aranyó

Carrer de Bolívia

Carrer de Bolívia
Carrer Bolívi

Pere IV

Fabra Media-TIC

Can Framis Museum

PARC DEL CENTRE DEL POBLENOU

MUHBA
Oliva Artés

Carrer de Tànger

C. de Sancho de Ávila

Av. Diagonal

C. Pere IV

Fluvià

C. dels Almogàvers

C. dels Almogàvers

Sala Razzmatazz

Carrer de Pallars

Pere IV

Carrer de Pallars

Carrer de Pallars

Bogatell

Carrer de Pujades

Llacuna

POBLE NOU

Poblenou

Carrer de Pujad

C. de Pujades

Carrer de Llull

Carrer de Llull

Carrer de Llull

Tío Che
Can Saladrigas

Carrer de

Ramon Turró

Doctor Trueta

Mercat de la Unió

Taulat
Plaça de Prim

Carrer del Perelló

CEMENTIRI DE L'EST

Carrer de Carmen Amaya

VILA OLÍMPICA

PARC DEL POBLENOU

Plaça dels Voluntaris
PARC DEL PORT OLÍMPIC

Hotel Arts
Arola
Frank's

Torre Mapfre

Plaça dels Campions
PARC DE LA NOVA ICARIA

Ronda del Litoral

Skatepark Mar Bella

Complex Esportiu Municipal Mar Bella

Frank Gehry's Fish Sculpture

Port Olímpic

Moll de Gregal

Platja Nova Icària

Platja del Bogatell

Platja de la Mar Bella

Avinguda Icària

Pg de Calvell

MEDITERRANEAN

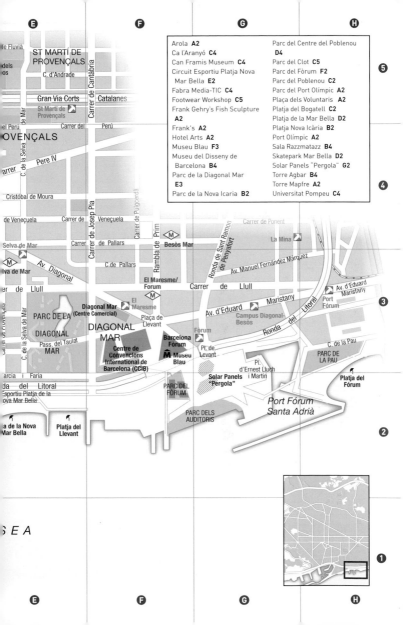

E

ST MARTÍ DE PROVENÇALS

C. d'Andrade

Gran Via Corts Catalanes

St Martí de Provençals

Carrer del Perú

PROVENÇALS

Pere IV

Cristóbal de Moura

de Venezuela   Carrer de   Venezuela

Selva de Mar   Carrer   de   Pallars

M
Iva de Mar

Av. Diagonal

C.de Pallars

El Maresme/ Forum

r   de   Llull

El Maresme

Diagonal Mar
(Centre Comercial)

PARC DE LA   Plaça de Llevant

DIAGONAL MAR

DIAGONAL MAR

Pass. del Taulat

Centre de Convencions International de Barcelona (CCIB)

Barcelona Fórum

M Museu Blau

rcia i   Faria

da   del   Litoral
sportiu Platja de la oya Mar Bella

a de la Nova Mar Bella   Platja del Llevant

SEA

F

C. de Cantàbria

Carrer del   Perú

Carrer de Josep Pla

Carrer de Puigcerdà

Rambla del Prim

Besòs Mar

Campus Diagonal-Besòs

Fórum

Pl. de Llevant

Solar Panels "Pergola"

PARC DEL FÒRUM

PARC DELS AUDITORIS

G

Arola **A2**	Parc del Centre del Poblenou
Ca l'Aranyó **C4**	**D4**
Can Framis Museum **C4**	Parc del Clot **C5**
Circuit Esportiu Platja Nova	Parc del Fòrum **F2**
Mar Bella **E2**	Parc del Poblenou **C2**
Fabra Media-TIC **C4**	Parc del Port Olímpic **A2**
Footwear Workshop **C5**	Plaça dels Voluntaris **A2**
Frank Gehry's Fish Sculpture	Platja del Bogatell **C2**
A2	Platja de la Mar Bella **D2**
Frank's **A2**	Platja Nova Icària **B2**
Hotel Arts **A2**	Port Olímpic **A2**
Museu Blau **F3**	Sala Razzmatazz **B4**
Museu del Disseny de	Skatepark Mar Bella **D2**
Barcelona **B4**	Solar Panels "Pergola" **G2**
Parc de la Diagonal Mar	Torre Agbar **B4**
E3	Torre Mapfre **A2**
Parc de la Nova Icaria **B2**	Universitat Pompeu **C4**

Carrer de Ponent

La Mina

Ronda de Sant Ramon de Penyafort

Av. Manuel Fernández Márquez

Carrer   de   Llull

Av. d'Eduard   Maristany

Av. d'Eduard Maristany

Port Fórum

Ronda   del   Litoral

C. de la Pau

PARC DE LA PAU

Pl. d'Ernest Lluch i Martín

Platja del Fórum

Port Fórum Santa Adrià

H

5

4

3

2

1

E   F   G   H

Sip up a sunset cocktail with a sea, and giant fish, view

There is no better way to end a day's sightseeing than sitting in the garden terrace of the **Hotel Arts**, sipping one of Barcelona's most creative cocktails, with endless views to the sea and to the glistening copper and gold mesh fish swimming in the sky over the marina. Frank Gehry's giant fish of interwoven steel strips has graced the marina of Vila Olímpica since the 1992 Olympic Games, when this whole area was regenerated.

The hotel has many eateries and bars. The flagship restaurant, **Arola** (map A2), is run by two-starred Michelin chef Sergi Arola, a disciple of superstar chefs Ferrán Adrià and Pierre Gagnaire, who puts his own twist into traditional tapas.

The bar **Frank's** (map A2) is headed by celebrity mixologist Diego Baud, Colorado-born but with Spanish roots. For several years he's been busily putting those roots back down in the gardens of the hotel where he grows ingredients for his alchemist-style creations. So there's a good chance that some of the lavender and nasturtium around you will end up in your cocktail. Savour your liquid masterpiece while sharing some modern tapas – think Iberian pork slices with Idiazabal cheese, apple, pistachios and chilli.

DJs add music to the sea-view deck every evening. Other food and drink events here include Vermouth & Tapas summer Sundays with the city's favourite apéritif woven into every cocktail imaginable, and live music, cocktails and culinary highs on Thursday nights.

Hotel Arts Barcelona; Carrer de la Marina, 19–21; tel: 932 21 10 00; www.hotelartsbarcelona.com; map A2

Make your own artisan sandals with a master shoemaker

Tucked away among the old factories of the Provençals del Poblenou near the Parc del Clot, the **Taller de Calzado** 'footwear workshop' is a space where you can learn to make your own shoes, whether you're a total beginner or advanced.

With all the tools and materials for manufacturing handmade shoes with quality finishes at your fingertips, you'll learn all the different processes involved from design to finish.

The small group courses are taught in Catalan, Spanish and English, and teacher Christian Romero also offers customised courses to help you achieve that perfect pair of *zapatos* with masterful precision.

Good craftsmanship requires time, so this is not one for those in a hurry. Even for the beginners' course *básico de iniciación* you'll need 18 hours to make a gorgeous artisan pair of women's flats choosing from various models – ballerinas, *merceditas* or loafers – and fine materials of various colours and textures. You will then be taught how to cut the leather soles and insoles, trim, assemble and polish.

In other longer courses you can learn how to make Oxfords and Bluchers, boots and sandals, sewing by hand and machine. Well-grounded pros can get into shoe design and create their own fantasy shoes from scratch in a free-reign workshop called *taller libre*.

Your new shoes in hand, or foot, wander through the district, laid out in the 1980s on land formerly occupied by ramshackle 19th-century factories and warehouses to accommodate the Vila Olímpica, the 1992 Olympic village. In the **Parc del Clot** (map C5), remnants of factories include stone arches from the old Renfe warehouses, Spain's national rail.

Carrer de la Llacuna 165–67 (entrance by side alley); tel: 933 09 71 87; contact Christian tallerdecalzado@tallerdecalzado.com; www.tallerdecalzado.com; map C5

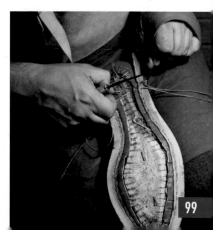

Scope out the city of tomorrow at 22@Barcelona

The former 19th-century working-class area of El Poblenou was once dubbed the 'Manchester of Catalonia' due to its textile industry and the style of industrial architecture, a fusion of Manchester-style iron structures with Catalan vaulting.

Since 2000 however, the Barcelona City Council has been steering it towards a dramatic new look – fitting for a place whose name means 'New Town'. The **22@Barcelona** urban renewal project is transforming some 400 disused or unproductive factories into a magnet for new activities, yet safeguarding their history under an Industrial Heritage Protection Plan.

Join **architour** (Carrer Sant Francesc, 63; tel: 93 8834 184;

www.architour.es) to get a fascinating glimpse of the evolving district. The four-hour architect-led visit takes in 17 sites, all contemporary developments often built around the old industrial chimneys to striking effect. Most of the old factory buildings have been converted into digital and knowledge centres but also social housing and art facilities.

Among them are the **Can Framis Museum** (Carrer Roc Boronat, 116–26; map C4) of the Fundació Vila Casas, a factory-turned-contemporary art foundation; the media and communication campus of the **Universitat Pompeu Fabra** (Carrer Roc Boronat, 138; map C4), housed in a former textile factory; and **Ca l'Aranyó** (map C4), a harmonious mix of old brick buildings and red screen-printed glass slats – all set around a new public square.

At the cube-shaped digital technology hub **Media-TIC** (Carrer Roc Boronat, 117; map F4) architect Enric Ruiz-Geli used a mesh structure of antique green steel covered with inflatable white bubbles. The translucent plastic shell is light sensitive and supposedly energy saving, though the building's constantly illuminated state, as alluring as it is, has cast doubt on that.

Discover an architectural urban oasis at the Parc de la Diagonal Mar

Also called Miralles Park, the **Parc de la Diagonal Mar** is a feat of the imagination by husband and wife team Enric Miralles and Benedetta Tagliabue. Sprawling along the waterfront, its twisting tubular sculptures spurt water out over an interior lake like a steel octopus of fantastical proportions.

Located 4km (2.5 miles) north of Barceloneta along the coast, it's almost as far as one can go without leaving Barcelona for Badalona.

Design Museum

At the **Museu del Disseny de Barcelona** (Plaça de les Glòries Catalanes, 37–38; tel 93 256 68 00; Tue–Sun 10am–8pm; map B4), discover fashion, product design, textile arts, period clothing, ceramics, graphic and decorative arts. The metal-clad structure designed by local firm MBM Arquitectes is a work of art in itself, jutting out its angular shape over an artificial lake.

And the far-out location is matched by the far-out architecture that lies within. The architects really pushed towards the heights of innovative, sustainable architecture with their 2002 oeuvre.

Occupying the site of a former factory, the 14-hectare park is divided into seven main areas including a large children's play area, an elevated walkway, a lake and a large central plaza, all connected by one theme – water.

The raised tubular structure that spiders its way through the park, coiling itself around suspended plant pots, is both art and innovative green technology, for it carries groundwater to irrigate the semi-tropical gardens. A green and organic artistic vision their famous compatriot Gaudí would be proud of.

Parc de la Diagonal Mar; Carrer de Llull, 362; map E3

Enjoy some fun in the sun on Barcelona's new beaches

An outdoor gym

The **Circuit Esportiu Passeig Marítim** (map E2) is a council-run, free outdoor gym on the El Poblenou waterfront. Enjoy working out on a range of fitness machines and equipment at several locations along El Poblenou and greater Sant Martí district: at the Platja de la Nova Icària, Platja del Bogatell, and Platja Nova Mar Bella.

Even in the 13th century when the old Roman city was surrounded by walls, the beaches of Barcelona remained free of fortifications. In the later Middle Ages, along-side numerous bids to create an artificial harbour, the city's beaches really began to take shape.

The urban regeneration prior to the 1992 Olympics led to major im-provements of the eastern beaches.

their cleanliness and leisure amenities are second to none: playgrounds, table-tennis tables, volleyball and basketball courts as well as beach exercise equipment (see box). Nova Icaria beach also has a dedicated zone for disabled people and those with reduced mobility, including a bathing support service to help them in and out of the water, and an amphibious chair.

The wide Passeig Maritim, with its separate cycling and walking lanes, continues east to the **Platja del Bogatell** (map C2). Join the body beautifuls on this golden stretch of sand. As well as being a great place to people-watch, it's also extremely family friendly with many amenities: sun loungers and beach umbrellas, a children's games area, drinks and ice-cream kiosks, bicycle parking areas, Wi-Fi, adapted showers and loos, and there are lifeguards and a police presence, and a beach information point (in English).

Further along, the Base Náutica Municipal de Barcelona on the **Platja de la Mar Bella** (map F2) rents sailing, surfing and windsurfing gear and kayaks, and has a large children's play area too – but be warned it is a nudist-friendly beach too.

Hinging on the construction of Vila Olímpica, coastal parklands, wide boardwalks and better seaside roads were built and the 'new beaches' as they're known came into being.

First in line is the **Platja de la Nova Icaria** (map B2) just after the Port Olimpíc Marina and roughly halfway along the city seafront. Not only are these beaches more peaceful than those downtown,

Walk in the parks of Vila Olímpica and El Poblenou

While the Parc de la Diagonal Mar (see page 101) might tick all the boxes on the Modernist front there are other parks in Poblenou to be enjoyed. Much closer to the marina, hotels and shops, you will find wonderful places to take shade, go for a jog or take the kids.

Starting at the **Parc del Port Olímpic** (map A2) and adjacent **Parc de la Nova Icaria** (map B2) the whole waterfront is a succession of parks and wide landscaped strips along the Avinguda del Litoral. A far cry from El Poblenou's industrial past.

The soft hills of the **Parc del Poblenou** (map C2) undulate along the coast between Bogatell and Mar Bella beaches, dotted with palm and pine trees and, strangely, some rusted maritime relics. Crisscrossed with pedestrian and bike paths, the park also boasts an athletics track and a sailing school.

Away from the waterfront on the Avinguda Diagonal is Barcelona's very own Central Park, the **Parc del Centre del Poblenou** (map D4). Capturing the post-industrial flavour of the neighbourhood, the young park (2008) is built around one of Poblenou's old mill buildings and industrial chimneys.

French architect Jean Nouvel took inspiration from Gaudí for this park with his curvilinear snaking perimeter wall, covered with flowering creepers and bougainvillea and punctuated with porthole-like openings. Then inside, the main garden is snail-shaped with spiralling-down Mediterranean bushes and shrubs. Dotted around are surging sculptures and trees, stylised metal seats, children's play areas and table tennis tables. In all there are some 1,000 tree species, which are gradually forming a canopy over the park.

Stand in between two giants and a fish at Port Olímpic

Alongside the Port Olímpic, the **Plaça dels Voluntaris** (map A2) was the ceremonial hub of the Olympic Village that housed the athletes competing in the 1992 Games.

An entirely new neighbourhood was built by the sea, setting in motion one of the city's greatest eras of urban renewal and architectural ingenuity. Stunning residential and office towers joined the old industrial chimneys as leading architects were chosen to regenerate the coastline.

Both a central roundabout and a public square, the Plaça dels Voluntaris is sandwiched by Barcelona's 'twin towers': the **Torre Mapfre** (map A2) and the **Hotel Arts Barcelona** (see page 98). The latter was erected at the heart of the Olympic Village to host the athletes prior to opening to the general public.

The duo of skyscrapers tower over Frank Gehry's huge woven fish

sculpture *Pez y Esfera* (Fish and Sphere; see page 98) and the port from an identical 144m (472ft), beating the Torre Agbar (see page 108) by about 10m (33ft). Currently the tallest skyscrapers in the city, they will be surpassed by the 172m (564ft) central tower of the Sagrada Família on its completion, which Barcelona building regulations prohibit any new buildings exceeding.

The garden strip of Volunteer's Square unfurls in a regimented line of greenery, former flag poles, and eye-catching sculptures – notably the highly expressionist *Marc* statue of a man adorned with strokes of colour poking through a large frame. A 1997 work by Barcelona-born sculptor Robert Llimós, it is a tribute to his late son Marc. The word also means picture frame in Catalan.

A Michelin treat

Enjoy some fine dining at the two Michelin starred **Enoteca** restaurant at Hotel Arts. Catalan chef Paco Perez's exquisite Mediterranean, seafood-oriented menu is matched by a stunning white-wood and glass décor and a vertical cellar of over 700 wines. Open Tue–Sat 7.30–10.30pm, Sat also 1.30–3.30pm.

Stroll around four continents then meet lions and dinosaurs at the Museu Blau

Jutting into the sea, the **Fòrum** area is a legacy of a world symposium in 2004 and now used for large-scale events.

Rising up among the budding hotels and retail outlets, the Plaça Leonardo Da Vinci at the entrance to the Fòrum is flanked by two iconic buildings: the spectacular glass cube of the Barcelona International Convention Centre by Josep Lluís Mateo and the triangular Fòrum Building by Swiss architects Jacques Herzog and Pierre de Meuron.

The latter houses the **Museu Blau**, Barcelona's natural science museum formerly in the Parc de la Ciutadella. Highlights include a permanent exhibition of planet earth and its history, a section exploring life from microbes to reproduction, a gallery of stuffed animals and one

of only two replicas in the world of a Prognatodon dinosaur. This is a very child-friendly museum with lots of interactive displays and tailored activities including a Science Nest at the weekend for the under 6s.

The fun continues outside in the botanical gardens, where you can stroll amongst five very distinct areas: the Mediterranean, Chile, California, South Africa and Australia.

Beyond the museum, the **Parc del Fòrum** (map F2) is Barcelona's newest seafront strip. Along the Grand Esplanade you will walk under the enormous solar panel **Pergola** (map G2), another symbol of Barcelona's renewable energy drive.

The Fòrum area is still a work in progress and fascinating to watch. Its eerie no man's land atmosphere has featured in many adverts. The marina will develop as more locals come to the area and the proposed new Diagonal-Besòs university campus building, centred on Zaha Hadid's Spiralling Tower, starts to take shape.

Museu Blau (Museu de Ciències Naturals); Plaça Leonardo da Vinci, 4-5; Parc del Fòrum; tel: 932566002; Tue–Sat 10am–7pm, Sun 10am–8pm; www.museuciencies.cat; map F3

Carve and flip like a true pro in El Poblenou's seafront skatepark

Dotted around El Poblenou's constantly evolving contemporary neo-industrial architecture, are several dedicated skateboarding zones big and small.

The largest is the **Skatepark Mar Bella**, stretching nearly 3,000 sq m (32,292 sq ft) on the seaside of Diagonal Mar i El Front Marítim del Poblenou. Opened in 2014, this the first of several planned.

The vast, curved park has different areas for skateboarders of varying skill levels, and for practicing different tricks. There's a street-skate area in the upper levels of the park, a long and smooth downhill run to the other end as well as a snake run. Then closer to Mar Bella beach there is a massive pool area, with a large bowl for experienced skaters and two small pools for beginners, and other multipurpose areas with ramps and jumps.

The park is open 24h so you can come here in the early evening when the summer's day temperatures have cooled down.

Skatepark Mar Bella; Avinguda del Litoral, 106; open 24h; map D2

Catch the kaleidoscopic colours of Torre Agbar at night

Following on from the post-Olympic Games urban regeneration programme, a new knowledge-based industrial district started to take shape in 2001 between the Plaça de les Glòries and the waterfront. Many key companies in ICT, medical technology, energy and media commissioned state-of-the-art skyscrapers by high-profile local and international architects, turning the area into a playground of daring contemporary architecture.

The **Torre Agbar** got the ball rolling when it was completed in 2005 as the headquarters of the water company Grupo Agbar. French architect Jean Nouvel's 144m (473ft) tall rocket-shaped landmark was intended to evoke a water tower, and its design was also a nod to Montserrat, a mountain outside Barcelona, and to Gaudí's Sagrada Família. Acclaimed by fellow architects as a 'a new cathedral', locals have given it rather more unflattering nicknames, one being *el supositori* ('the suppository'). In 2017, the tower was renamed Torre Glòries when it was purchased by another company. Time will tell if that name catches on.

For his tower, Nouvel harnessed the sun and groundwater to reduce energy consumption in the building. Clad in coloured glass panels that can be tilted at different angles to capture solar energy, the space between them facilitates natural ventilation in the building.

But the tower truly comes in to its own at night when it reflects 40 varying shades of blue red and white like a giant kaleidoscope – a perfect example of when architecture becomes a dazzling spectacle.

Torre Agbar (Torre Glòries); Avinguda Diagonal, 211; map B4

Party like it's 1999 at Razzmatazz

The cavernous **Sala Razzmatazz** is Barcelona's ultimate live music venue.

Housed in a former factory in El Poblenou, it's actually five clubs in one: The Razzclub, The Loft, Lolita, The Pop Bar and The Rex Room dedicated respectively to indie rock concerts, techno shows, chilled pop, electro and disco acts.

Opened in 2000, this was the first club in Spain to schedule happenings in five different spaces every day of the week.

Few Barcelonans would disagree with it branding itself as 'a flagship of the culture and leisure scene on a national and international scale' and some go as far as proclaiming it 'club of the decade'.

It certainly caters to a wide audience – you can come here to listen to the local newcomers or big-name acts or bop the night away to electronic dance music. David Byrne, Coldplay, Orbital, Pulp, The Strokes, Blur, Belle and Sebastian,

Richie Hawtin, Jeff Mills, Paul Kalkbrenner, Justice or Skrillex, are some of the performers and DJ's to have played here. And for The Arctic Monkeys, Franz Ferdinand, Cut Copy and The Gossip this was their first big international gig.

The multi-space club also hosts mega parties, private dinners, fashion shows and galas so best to check its calendar of events well in advance to make sure you don't miss out.

Sala Razzmatazz; Carrer dels Almogàvers, 122; tel: 93 320 8200; www.salarazzmatazz.com; map B4

Concerts a gogo

Also watch out for major international concerts and ballet at the Auditori Fòrum, the concert hall of the International Conventions Centre within the Fòrum Building (www.ccib.es/spaces/forum-auditorium).

L'EIXAMPLE

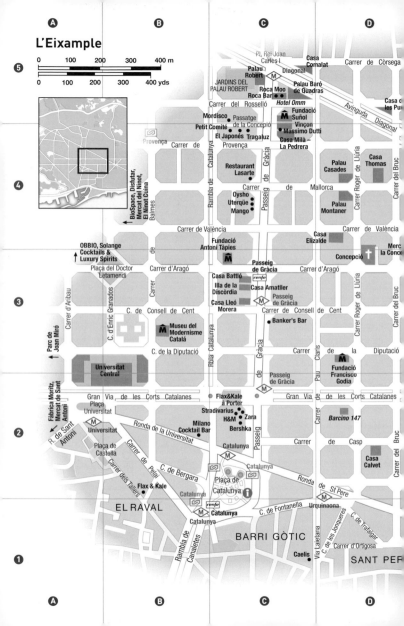

L'Eixample

5

| 0 | 100 | 200 | 300 | 400 m |
| 0 | 100 | 200 | 300 | 400 yds |

A   **B**   **C**   **D**

Pl. Rei Joan Carles I

Diagonal

Casa Comalat

Carrer de Còrsega

Palau Robert

JARDINS DEL PALAU ROBERT

Roca Moo

Roca Bar

Palau Baró de Quadras

Casa de les Pu

Carrer del Rosselló

Avinguda Diagonal

Hotel Omm

Mordisco

Passatge de la Concepció

Petit Comité

El Japonés   Tragaluz

Fundació Suñol

Vinçon

Massimo Dutti

Casa Milà – La Pedrera

Provença

Carrer de Provença

Restaurant Lasarte

Palau Casades

Carrer Roger de Llúria

Casa Thomas

Carrer del Bruc

Carrer   de   Mallorca

Oysho

Uterqüe

Mango

Palau Montaner

Carrer de València

Casa Elizalde

Carrer de València

OBBIO, Solange Cocktails & Luxury Spirits

Fundació Antoni Tàpies

Passeig de Gràcia

Concepció

Merc la Conce

Plaça del Doctor Letamendi

Carrer d'Aragó

Carrer d'Aragó

Carrer Roger de Llúria

Carrer del Bruc

Casa Battló

Illa de la Discòrdia

Casa Lleó Morera

Casa Amatller

Passeig de Gràcia

Carrer de Consell de Cent

C. de Consell de Cent

Museu del Modernisme Català

Banker's Bar

C. de la Diputació

Carrer de la Diputació

Universitat Central

Passeig de Gràcia

Fundació Francisco Godia

Gran Via de les Corts Catalanes

Gran Via de les Corts Catalanes

Plaça Universitat

Flax&Kale à Porter

Stradivarius

Milano Cocktail Bar

H&M

Zara

Bershka

Barcino 147

Universitat

Ronda de la Universitat

Carrer de Casp

Plaça de Castella

Casa Calvet

Carrer del

Carrer de Bergara

Catalunya

Plaça de Catalunya

Ronda de St Pere

EL RAVAL

Flax & Kale

C. de Fontanella

Urquinaona

Catalunya

BARRI GÒTIC

Carrer d'Ortigosa

Caelis

SANT PER

Visit a Modernista chocolatier's house then buy an edible memento

The **Casa Amatller**, designed by Josep Puig i Cadafalch, is one of a trio of Modernista buildings standing side-by-side on the Passeig de Gràcia called Illa de la Discòrdia (or 'Block of Discord') due to their conflicting styles. It is sandwiched between Gaudí's Casa Batlló (see page 118) and Domènech i Montaner's Casa Lleó Morera.

All three were makeovers of existing buildings, but the Casa Amatller came first. In 1898, chocolatier and industrialist Antoni Amatller Costa commissioned Catalan architect-politician Puig to overhaul the existing building. Amatller lived here with his daughter and he was also a keen photographer so you can check the veracity of some of the room recreations against his black and whites on the walls.

Considered one of the most revolutionary and striking edifices of its time, Casa Amatller combines a neo-Gothic, Moorish-influenced interior with a Dutch-gabled facade.

The takes in the entire house, from its splendid stained-glass and tiled hallways, candelabra-lit salons, to exquisitely furnished bedrooms and antechambers with Moorish design elements and painted ceilings. Precious oak and walnut wood furnishings fill the house. Moorish decorative elements are visible everywhere: tiles, horseshoe arches, fluted columns, elaborately veneered parquet floors and multi-hued leadlight screens.

Highlights include the living room, sporting the original 1898 wallpaper from a collection presented in Paris by the designer Isadore Leroy.

In the large dining room, to evoke the atmosphere of bygone urban palaces and gain ceiling height, Puig replaced the original iron beams and top slabs with wooden beams supported by brick inlay wall brackets. Decorative *sgraffito* mouldings

More chocolate...

Barcelona has a thriving organic and eco-responsible lifestyle and there are many organic shops in l'Eixample. As you head towards the Sagrada Família you'll come across **Veritas** (Passeig de Sant Joan, 144; map F5), where you can stock up on fine olive oils, conserves and tapenades, savoury snacks and sardines. They also have an incredible local chocolate selection: the milk *Xocolata Amb Llet* from Barcelona chocolatier Simón Coll with its classic maritime wrapper and from Blanxart, a Barcelona confectionery and chocolate shop, an earthy Ghanaian dark chocolate and raw vanilla-flavoured variety. Other sweet treats include *catànies*, chocolate-covered Catalan almonds, nutty *galetas* (biscuits), *melindros* (ladyfingers) and many varieties of *torró* (nougat).

on the walls and ceilings add to the pomp. This is the hub of the house with its massive stone and sculpture-hemmed fireplace, glazed polished marble floors and late Gothic-style furniture, crowned by mighty stained-glass and wrought-iron candelabra.

Amatller wanted the latest technology in his home, but due to frequent electricity failures all the lights had backup key-opening gas lamps with champagne flute-like burners and coloured leadlight features.

Before leaving, drop by the ground-floor shop and tearoom of **Chocolate Amatller**, a house founded in 1800. The retro bars make for a perfect souvenir of your visit.

To sleep in arty surroundings yourself, book a room at nearby **Barcino147**, a boutique B&B with airs of an art gallery. Its lavish apartments are filled with antiques and local art selected by the owner, an artist and art collector who studied like Picasso at La Llotja (see page 70).

Casa Amatller; Passeig de Gràcia, 41; tel: 934 617 460; daily 10am–6pm; www.amatller.org; map C3
Barcino 147; Gran Via de les Corts Catalanes, 662; tel: 607-379101; www.barcelonabarcino147.com

Eye up a Modernista first then tap into some Tàpies art

When searching for a permanent home for his works in 1984, the Catalan painter and sculptor Antoni Tàpies came across a rundown but pioneering building in the Eixample. The former publishing house headquarters of Montaner i Simon, with its exposed brick facade and wrought-iron frame, was one of the city's first Modernista buildings.

A Montaner himself, this was young architect Lluis Domenech i Montaner's first Modernista project, and for the facade he fused the industrial style of the building with classical and Moorish decorative elements.

The facade is crowned by Tàpies's bold sculpture *Núvol i Cadira* ('Cloud and Chair'), a wire mesh designed to lift the building's height to the level of the adjoining houses on either side. With his strong allegiances to Catalanist republicanism, and love of Nietzsche and Thomas Mann, the work embodies Tàpies's vision of his art as a meditation on 'the void'.

Born in Barcelona in 1923, his interest in contemporary art was sparked as a teenager seeing works by Picasso, Mondrian, Kandinsky and Miró. During the Spanish Civil War he taught himself drawing and painting, and aged 20

he spent a lengthy convalescence from lung disease drawing copies of Van Gogh and Picasso works.

His **Fundació Antoni Tàpies** is a showcase for some 300 of his works as well as temporary exhibitions, in a décor of crisp white pillars offset by a raw ironwork ceiling. In the basement former printing press rooms, you will find the artist's private collection including works by some of the greats who inspired him.

Fundació Antoni Tàpies; Aragó, 255; tel: 934 870 315; Tue–Sun 10am–7pm (booking required for guided visits); www.fundaciotapies.org; map C3

Chill out with a smooth cocktail at L'Eixample's best jazz bars

L'Eixample has a bevy of sophisticated post-work winding down establishments, elegant late night bars and smooth jazz joints open to the small hours.

Located in the trendy L'Antiga Esquerra de l'Eixample district, **Solange Cocktails & Luxury Spirits** (Carrer d'Aribau, 143; daily 6pm–2.30am) is a voluptuously swish cocktail bar, from its Modernist entrance down to the Chesterfield banquettes, vintage velvet and brass and glass tables. It's named after a Bond Girl in *Casino Royale*, and the owner's Bond bewitchment is clear to see in the décor and the class act of classic cocktails and top-shelf spirits. The team's bespoke 'cocktails d'auteur' often see it rated among the world's best bars.

For a plush hotel bar experience, head to **Banker's Bar** at the Mandarin Oriental (Passeig de Gràcia, 38–40; Sun–Wed 5pm–1am, Thu–Sat until 3am; map C3). As the name suggests, you will be sipping your raspberry and goji berry Bellini in a bank vault, decked with old bank safes. Themed jazz nights top up the glamour.

Red sofas, dim cinematic lighting and white columns greet you at the **Milano Cocktail Bar** (Ronda de la Universitat, 35; daily noon–3am; map B2) in L'Eixample's Sant Antoni neighbourhood. True to setting, the cocktails are movie-themed and there are nightly live music sessions. The jazz & blues vibe make it a magnet for writers and artists.

Jazz, soul, funk and R&B have found a glamourous setting in the mellow surrounds of Hotel Omm's **Lobby Roca Bar** (map C5) with live music sessions by local and visiting artists at 8.30pm (Mon–Sat).

See the world in curves at the Casa Batlló

While the nearby Casa Milà (see page 122) shows off Gaudí's love of curves mostly on the outside and at the top, the **Casa Batlló** embraces them all the way up its the six storeys, inside and out. There is almost no straight line in sight, from the curved hallways and stairwells to the furniture, doorways and undulating balconies.

Textile baron Josep Batlló commissioned Gaudí to remodel his house. Completed in 1906, it is considered the ultimate Gaudí masterpiece and was declared a World Heritage site in 2005.

The blue-green ceramic facade is dazzling, with its sensuously curving windows and scale-like roof reminiscent of a sea-monster (some suggests it depicts St George, patron saint of Barcelona, and the dragon).

The extraordinary decoration continues inside, from Batlló's office, through grand public rooms, including the furniture designed by Gaudí for the Batlló family, to the spectacular roof. But as fanciful as his architecture was, it was also uncannily practical. Ahead of his time, Gaudí came up with ingenious building solutions for ventilation or lighting which always had an attractive decorative finish. The attic of the Casa Batlló is where his idea of natural ventilation reached an artful peak with the milk-white walls 'sliced open like fish gills'.

Rooftops were the centre of the Gaudí cosmos. They had to be spectacular, never mundane. This is exemplified on the rooftop of the Casa Batlló, with extraordinary tiled chimneys. The radial and spiral forms of the sculptures coupled with the use of polychrome mosaic tiles create a wonderful kaleidoscopic effect.

Gaudí used recycled pieces of broken ceramics and glass and materials from demolished buildings to decorate his new works, which conceptually were a forerunner to the sustainable practices of today.

The Casa Batlló now also organises theatrical visits and from June until September night visits accompanied by live jazz music on the roof. You can also book an early-bird visit (8.30am) if you want to avoid the crowds. See website for details.

Casa Batlló; Passeig de Gràcia, 43; 934 880 666; www.casabatllo.es; daily 9am–9pm; map C3

Brunch and browse in newly restored art nouveau markets

A giant of terracotta- and gold-hued ironwork and glass topped by an octagonal stained-glass cupola, the market hall of the **Mercat de Sant Antoni** spreads over an entire block of L'Eixample's hipster Sant Antoni neighbourhood.

Over the main entrance, spot a decorative insignia featuring the Barcelona coat of arms, crowned by a bat and the year of construction, 1882. Designed by Antoni Rovira i Trias in exemplary Catalan art nouveau modernist style, the market underwent major remodelling before reopening in 2017.

Come here on a weekday to soak in the ambience generated by some 250 stallholders selling vegetables, fruit and fish indoors, clothing, shoes and other goods outdoors. On Sundays, locals gather to buy second-hand books and collector magazines and swap stamps.

For a pre- or post-market bite stop by one of the eateries of the **Carrer del Parlament**: cutesy **Cafè Cometa** (20) for Serrano ham sandwiches, coffee and carrot cake or a chai latte and vegan treats; or the **Federal Café** (39) for all things egg.

Higher up, in L'Antiga Esquerra de l'Eixample, the **Mercat del Ninot** is another recently restored small but charming market. The *ninot* (wooden doll) salvaged from a ship still graces the entrance. This is a great place to stock up on dried fruit and nuts.

Cooking up a storm in its open kitchen, **El Ninot Cuina** serves market-fresh chargrilled clams with tomato and chilli, salted cod and haricot bean salad or Murcian-style rice with vegetables and pulses in a pared-down Scandi décor.

Mercat de Sant Antoni; Carrer del Comte d'Urgell, 1; Mon–Thu 7am–2.30pm and 5.30–8.30pm, Fri–Sat 7am–8.30pm, Sun 10am–3pm
Mercat del Ninot; Carrer de Mallorca, 133–57; Mon–Fri 9am–8pm, Sat until 2pm
El Ninot Cuina; Carrer Casanova 133; Mon–Sun breakfast and lunch, Tue–Sat dinner

Splurge on some Michelin-starred fare from the city's most celebrated chefs

Barcelona has the most Michelin-starred establishments in the whole of Spain and L'Eixample is where you'll find nearly half of them. Chef Martín Berasategui's **Restaurant Lasarte** was awarded three stars in 2017, making him the most Michelin-decorated chef in the country. So reserve well in advance to sample his seafood-heavy, Basque but French-influenced haute cuisine.

Disfrutar means 'enjoy' and that's exactly what you'll be doing at one-star **Disfrutar**. The trio of chefs all come from the famous El Bulli restaurant so be prepared for dining theatre. The 20- and 30-dish tasting menus are served in ceramic-tiled dining room redolent of a fishing village.

With the Roca brothers at the helm, one-star design-centric Roca Moo fits perfectly into the post-Modernista stone and wood décor of Hotel Omm. On the tasting menus, playful twists on Catalan cooking such as plankton gnocchi in sea pesto, a golden egg in a caramelised shell are prepared before your eyes and served with matching wines.

Caelis's young chef Romain Fornell mixes his French and Catalan roots into his cuisine, with a modern and minimalist twist, just like the décor. Dishes to try are tuna cannelloni and baked Iberian bacon.

Restaurant Lasarte; Carrer Mallorca, 259; tel: 934 453 242; www.restaurantlasarte. com; Tue–Sat 1.30–3.30pm and 8.30–11pm; map C4
Disfrutar; Carrer Villarroel, 163; tel: 933 486 896; Tue–Sat 1–2.30pm and 8–9.30pm
Roca Moo; Carrer del Rosselló, 265; tel: 934 454 000; www.hotelomm.com; Tue–Sat 1.30–3.30pm and 8–10.30pm; map C5
Caelis; Via Laietana, 49 (at Hotel Ohla Barcelona); tel: 935 101 205; www.caelis. com; Tue 8–10.30pm. Wed -Sat 1.30–3.30pm and 8–10.30pm; map C1

Giggle at the moustache-like balconies and be spooked out by witch-scarers at the Casa Milà

Commonly called 'La Pedrera' (stone quarry) after its rippling grey stone facade, the **Casa Milà** exemplifies Gaudí's love of natural motifs and organic shapes.

Casa Milà was commissioned by industrialist-politician Pere Milà i Camps and his wife Rosario Sergimon as their private residence, and took six years to build from 1906. It is one of Gaudí's three biggest residential masterpieces along with the Casa Calvet and the Casa Batlló (see page 118), all on the Passeig de Gràcia.

From the main courtyard, the typical Gaudí light-filled building surges up five floors, its multi-hued inner walls decked with dozens of curved windows, each sporting moustache-like intricate wisps of black ironwork.

The visit of this Unesco-listed site takes in a show flat recreated in the Modernista style, the attic, a first-floor exhibition space and the sculptured roof terrace.

The show flat is decorated as it would have been when the building was first occupied with lavish but solidly furnished salons and a sober kitchen. A maritime theme is carried through with large, wavy expanses of plaster, spiralled patterns, sea-snail and sea-flora reliefs.

The cavernous vaulted attic, with its fine 300 catenary brick arches, was used as a laundry room and for storage. It now houses an exhibition on Gaudí's work including models of La Pedrera from every angle, and of Park Güell. A video shows how the Casa Milà was part of Barcelona's growth and modernisation in the 1920s in the lead up to the Universal Exposition of 1929.

Reach the rooftop, to a mind-boggling moonscape of otherworldly forms and surprising features

and evil-looking chimney sculptures, inspired by medieval knights, that were dubbed 'witch-scarers'. For Gaudí, conventional rooftops were intolerably boring and ugly. 'The way buildings are topped are like bald heads without a single hair,' he once quipped.

The rooftop is the location of Casa Milà's summer jazz nights, where you sip a glass of cava, listen to a live band and enjoy the amazing view. You can also book an early-bird visit (8.30am) if you want to avoid the crowds. See website for details.

At home among L'Eixample's Modernista gems, is nearby **Hotel Omm**, whose facade is a contemporary, almost futuristic take on Casa Milà's curved exterior windows courtesy of architect Juli Capella.

Casa Milà–La Pedrera; Passeig de Gràcia, 92; tel: 902 202 138; www.lapedrera.com; daily 9am–8.30pm and 9–11pm; map C4 Hotel Omm; www.hotelomm.com; Carrer Del Rosselló, 265; tel: 93 445 40 00; map C5

Eat, drink and shop at a historic beer emporium

What do you get when you take a Frenchman from brasserie-laden Alsace and transport him to Barcelona? The answer is **Fàbrica Moritz**, the city's most famous brewery founded in 1856 by Louis Moritz.

Open almost round the clock its drinking and dining zones are spread over three floors. Enter another Frenchman, architect Jean Nouvel, who orchestrated the conversion, taking care not only to preserve but highlight the old bricks, adding vertical gardens and big window panes to give the impression of space.

Enjoy a craft beer on tap from the on-site microbrewery, next to the glass-encased art-like copper vats. The Moritz Beer Lab is constantly creating new ephemeral beers alongside the classic favourites so you will be spoilt for choice.

The Brewery Bar has an open kitchen and the city's longest bar. Here you can graze on unusual tapas mixing Alsace and Spanish flavours.

The cheekily named Easy Peasy and What the F*** menus were created by gastronomic director Jordi Vilà.

Afterwards you can explore round the old brewery and the pool-sized stone vat, now replaced by shiny copper ones. Downstairs is a design marvel of glass and sculptural lighting, home to wine bar **Bistrot de Vins** with a 700-strong wine list and to high-end restaurant **Louis 1856**.

Before leaving you might want to shop for Moritz-inspired gifts, from vintage posters to jewellery and shoes. Custom-made by local artists and furniture designers, many feature the company's trademark colour, banana yellow. And there is also a brewery bakery where you can buy some delicious beer bread.

Fàbrica Moritz; Ronda Sant Antoni, 39; tel: 934 26 00 50; Mon–Sun 7.30am–3am; www.moritz.com
Louis 1856; Wed–Sun 1.30–3.30pm and 8–11pm; tel: 93 425 37 70; www.louis1856.com

Enjoy some music and Miró where the city's slaughterhouse once stood

A fascinating cityscape bordering the Barcelona Sants train station, La Nova Esquerra de L'Eixample developed, as its name suggests, more recently than the other five barrios which make up the vast L'Eixample. It is home to the **Parc de Joan Miró**, one of the first urban parks created in the post-Franco era.

Miró's legacy is visible in the shape of his 22 m (70ft)-high statue *Dona i Ocell* (Woman and Bird), unveiled in 1983, just a few months before he died. The glazed-tile bird in bold Miró Mediterranean blue, red and yellow is striking in its simple setting on a small island in the middle of a reflecting pool.

All around it is a jigsaw layout of pergolas, pathways, bridges, and parterres of pines and evergreen oaks, encircling a central square. There are vast lawns where locals enjoy a picnic or a spot of sunbathing and there are great, shaded, playgrounds for kids to run wild in.

The two-tiered parc has a grisly nickname: 'park of the slaughterhouse' – *de l'Escorxador* – because of the abattoir that once stood here.

The park is one of the main hosts of the *Música als Parcs* programme of some 50 free summer concerts held across the city's green spaces. Plan it right and you'll enjoy a performance by quality young performers – soloists, jazz ensembles and orchestras – rigorously selected by a jury.

Parc de Joan Miró; Carrer d'Aragó, 2

Industrial park

In the Sants neighbourhood is another interesting garden conversion, the **Parc de l'Espanya Industrial** on the site of a former textile factory. The layout is very theatrical, with an amphitheatre around a rowing lake, canals, nine lighthouse towers and classical and contemporary sculptures, including a giant dragon doubling as a children's slide.

125

Take a culinary journey down gourmet street

One of L'Eixample's grid-design features are passageways running through the inner part of a block. These quiet *passatges* offer some respite from the surrounding commercial buzz and traffic.

The lovely **Passatge de la Concepió** (map C4) off the Passeig de Gràcia has a flourish of designer eateries offering fresh, innovative fare. The unfailing successful Grupo Tragaluz (www.grupo tragaluz.com) has established a little colony here, though all its restaurants are gastronomically and architecturally unique.

Mordisco (10; map C5), meaning 'nibble', was the group's first address, opening in the mid-1980s in a converted 19th-century house with period plaster ceilings, milky white walls and a balustrade wooden staircase. The main restaurant, set in a bucolic tree-kissed conservatory, also has a little deli in case you want to take some of the market-fresh delicacies home.

Young sibling **El Japonés** (5; map C4) combines the group's trademark mix of arresting décor and funky food, serving up fresh takes on Japanese classics and Asian fusion dishes such as Yakisoba noodles with omelette and ham in a red-hued dining room.

In the same building but up a loft stairway flanked with graphic art, is the group's flagship restaurant: **Tragaluz** (map C4), one of the city's first designer restaurants. Its name, meaning 'skylight', says it all. The open kitchen and vast dining room are topped by an impressive slanting glass roof giving the feel that you on a sunlit terrace. Order some artichokes with black Catalan

sausage, grilled Galician octopus, cuttlefish black rice or wild turbot in cardamom acid cream and some sparkling Gramona Cava and sit back to enjoy the views. For dessert, try the fluffy French toast-like caramelised *torrija* with homemade vanilla ice cream.

Break free from the group's grips at Nandu Jubany's gastronomic Michelin-starred **Petit Comité** (13; map C4), specialising in traditional Catalan fare like cod fritters or deep-fried calamari.

To see where a lot of the fresh produce on offer in this passageway comes from, stroll 15 minutes to the eponymous **Mercat de la Concepció** (Carrer d'Aragó, 313–17; map D4/3). The 1888 market is another creation of Antoni Rovira and Trias, of Sant Antoni and Barceloneta markets fame (see pages 120 and 91).

127

Attend a summer night's concert in the Jardins del Palau Robert

At the crossroads of the busy Avinguda Diagonal and the top end of the Passeig de Gràcia, enter the gardens of the **Palau Robert**, a cool haven in midsummer and host to a vibrant summer nights' programme of free concerts, the *Nits d'estiu musicals*.

Jazz, flamenco, sea shanties, opera, blues and Catalan pop-rock performances are held among the exotic flourish of pagoda, plane and Judas trees, cypresses, magnolias, large-leaved limes, Seville orange trees and evergreen Chinese thuja.

A typical garden of a 19th-century bourgeois mansion garden of Eixample, two gravel paths wind among the vegetation. The stainless-steel and iron moon sculpture with a red lectern is called *La lluna*, 'the Moon', created by philanthropic artist Kiku Mistu in 2001 as part of an educational project called *El llenguatge de les flors*, 'The Language of Flowers'. Inside is a poem in Braille.

The petite neoclassical Palau Robert was the home of a French nobleman and financier, the Marquis de Robert, before becoming a cultural headquarters for Catalan government administrators during the Civil War. Today its marbled interiors are home to the Catalan tourist office and to temporary exhibitions focusing on Catalan regional history and culture.

Watch out for more free *Niu d'estiu* activities at various locations from Casa Milà–La Pedrera to the Museu Blau.

Jardins del Palau Robert; Passeig de Gràcia, 107; map C5

Stroll and shop along the elegant Passeig de Gràcia

One of Barcelona's most important avenues, the **Passeig de Gràcia** is also its most elegant. This wide, tree-lined avenue is packed with Modernista masterpieces, palatial hotels and tree-shaded cafés. Along with the Avinguda Diagonal and Gran Via de les Corts Catalans, it is one of three major boulevards created by Ildefons Cerdà in his 1860 redesign of L'Eixample, widening it by 60m (200ft).

Enjoy strolling on the ample pavements, stopping to admire the beautiful wrought-iron streetlamps incorporated with mosaic benches often mistaken as Gaudí creations but in fact designed by Pere Falqués i Urpi in 1906.

The Passeig de Gràcia is also a shopping heaven. Housed in its modernist mansions and grand arcades, are beautiful shops pitching Benetton alongside Prada.

All the Spanish-born Inditex labels are here: **Bershka** (7; map C2), **Stradivarius** (11; map C2), **Zara** (16; map C2), **Oysho** (67; map C4), and the shoe store of **Uterqüe** (65 bis; map C4), Zara's posh sister.

The most spectacular is the new **Massimo Dutti** flagship store (96; map C4) opened in the restored 1898-built Casa Ramón Casas, a jewel of Catalan Modernism. The shop is also very high-tech. As well as Wi-Fi and self-checkout it sports 'buyable windows' which you zap with your iOS app, and interactive fitting rooms where the garments you're trying on appear on touch screens, allowing you to call up information or request a different size. For refreshment, head to the vintage van-café in the outdoor patio.

The first ever store of Zara competitor **Mango** is also here (65; map C4), opened in 1984. **H&M** has a four-storey emporium (11; map C2) offering all the collections under one roof as well as healthy food and juice bar **Flax&Kale à Porter**. The main **Flax & Kale** restaurant is located a few hundred meters/yards away (Carrer des Tallers, 748; map B2).

Passeig de Gràcia; map C2–C5

Get to grips with Gaudí's vision at the Sagrada Família museum

The **Sagrada Família** is extraordinary to behold – a symbol of Barcelona for most – with its forest of interior columns and stained glass which even the grimmest weather couldn't subdue. But once you've taken it all in, the museum below will unravel mysteries and enhance your insights into what made Gaudí really tick.

It was the director of city's art museums, Joaquim Folch i Torres who, after Gaudí's death in 1926, suggested establishing a museum in the architect's studio workshop to preserve and promote his work. And you can really feel Gaudí's soul here, for at the time he was run over by a tram (ignored by all the

passers-by as they mistook him for a tramp), he had almost relinquished his Park Güell quarters for his atelier here.

Gaudí apparently hated drawings and thought of innovative techniques to mentally map out his creations, notably the use of scale models made of chains hung from a ceiling or made of strings with weights attached.

The museum contains several models of his works. A replica of the string model of the church at the Colònia Güell is a favourite. The original, 4m (13ft)-high, was a prototype made from strings with small bags full of gun shells for ballast. There are of course also models of the Sagrada Família, under construction since 1882 and expected to be finally completed by 2026.

But it's the new 'Inspired by nature' section, a vast space opened in 2017, which reveals how important observing and analysing nature was in the development of Gaudí's organic architectural style.

His appreciation of nature can be seen in all his masterpieces: from the snail-shell spiral staircase at the Casa Milà to the ceiling swirls at the Casa Batlló, inspired by the descent of a winged seed from a Robina tree. And in the conical curves and hyperbolas of the central nave of the Sagrada Família with its tree-like pillars and branching columns rising up to the roof. 'The intimacy and depth is that of a wood, which will be the interior of the Temple of the Sagrada Família' Gaudi said.

In Gaudí's architecture nature met science – it was all about geometry and poetry. For example he used arches for their unbeatable mechanical properties and beauty but decorated them with patterns 'like branches of the oleander'. The displays are thematically displayed: 'The exuberance of nature', 'The geometry of nature' and 'The great forest and mineral crystals'.

As you leave the basilica take a quick stroll through one of the squares on either side of it: the **Plaça Sagrada Família** (map G4) and the **Plaça Gaudí** (map G/H4), whose pond was designed to reflect the incomplete modernist temple. Gaudí of course would have done the same. For inspiration's sake.

Sagrada Família and Museum;
Carrer de Mallorca, 401; tel: 935 132
060; Nov–Feb 9am–6pm, Mar 9am–7pm,
Apr–Sept 9am–8pm, Oct 9am–7pm;
www.sagradafamilia.org; map G4

GRÀCIA AND BEYOND

Head to the hills at sunset for a top view of the city from a Civil War bunker

For an off-the-beaten-path panoramic view of the city, head to the El Carmel neighbourhood and the viewpoint (*mirador*) up the **Turó de la Rovira** (map F3) hill, which for some surpasses that of the adjacent Turó de les Tres Creus hill in Parc Güell.

The Rovira hill, reaching 262m (860ft), is taller than its famous neighbour and it is topped by massive bunkers which you can climb onto. The Bunkers del Carmel were a strategic defence site during the Spanish Civil War, used as anti-aircraft batteries to defend the city from bombings.

The 360° views from here sweep in la Sagrada Família, 2.5km (1.5 miles) away as the crow flies, and everything beyond.

This makes for a very romantic spot, and couples come here at sunset with a bottle of red and picnic provisions to make the most of the spectacle. Besides sunset is really the only time to come here as it gets extremely hot in the summer on this exposed hilltop.

Bunkers del Carmel; Turó de la Rovira; Carrer de Marià Lavèrnia; El Carmel; map G3

Discover the exquisite Modernista hospital turned art gallery

The Unesco-listed Art Nouveau Site of the **Recinte Modernista de Sant Pau** is another gem in the legacy of Modernista maestro Lluis Domènech i Montaner, of Palau de la Música fame (see page 67).

Montaner built the forward-thinking complex between 1905 and 1930 as a garden city for nursing the sick. A recent makeover turned one of Europe's foremost art nouveau ensembles into an indoor-outdoor art gallery, a showcase for the applied arts. It is also a knowledge hub, acting as the headquarters for many international organisations, including the Global University Network for Innovation and the United Nations University Institute on Globalization, Culture and Mobility.

The exhibition space in the Sant Salvador Pavilion takes visitors on a journey through the history of medicine at one of Europe's oldest healthcare institutions, which evolved from Barcelona's first hospital, La Santa Creu, opened in El Raval in 1401 and relocated here in the late 19th century. On display are medical equipment and paraphernalia and the upper floor is dedicated to the genius of Montaner.

The best way to visit the building's exteriors is to follow the Art Nouveau Site trail: taking in the domes, roofs, sculptures, mosaics and stained-glass windows, before heading underground through the connecting passageways. The recommended route varies a little depending on the use being made of the spaces but you can get all the content on your smartphone through the CloudGuide app.

Recinte Modernista de Sant Pau; Carrer de Sant Antoni Maria Claret, 167; tel: 935 537 801; www.santpaubarcelona.org; Mon–Sat 10am–4.30pm, Sun 10am–2.30pm; map H1

Delve into the mysteries of a medieval medicinal garden at the world's largest Gothic cloister

Pedralbes, from the Latin *petras albas* (white stones), was the site chosen in 1327 by Queen Elisenda de Montcada to found a monastery for the Order of Saint Clare, which lived here until the 1930s. This is to this day one of the most peaceful corners of the city.

Some 6km (3.7 miles) southwest of the city centre, the **Monestir de Pedralbes** boasts a magnificent three-storey Gothic cloister, considered the largest of its kind.

The two ground-floor galleries contain 26 columns of Girona limestone, decorative leaves on its arches, and the wooden ceiling beams are painted with royal heraldry red and gold. The chapel, refectory, dormitory and other abbey rooms provide an insight into the day-to-day life of the nuns.

Outside is a recreated medieval medicinal garden flourishing with dozens of healing herbs. Tapping into Ancient Greek and Roman medicine, as well Arab-Islamic culture, the nuns here turned to nature for therapeutic properties cultivating plants to cure their sick. They got their knowledge from medieval writings on health and healing by German mystic and abbess, Hildegard of Bingen, author of the 11th-century tome *Physica*, and a Catalan translation of *The Book of Simple Medicines* by the Andalusian physician Ibn al-Wafid.

The 'Plants, Remedies and Apothecaries' exhibition extends through the former pharmacy and infirmary.

Monestir de Pedralbes; Baixada del Monestir, 9; tel 932 563 434; Apr–Sept: Tue–Fri 10am–5pm, Sat until 7pm, Sun until 8pm, Oct–Mar: Tue–Fri 10am–2pm, Sat–Sun 10am–5pm; www. monestirpedralbes.bcn.cat; map A/B4

Revisit Gràcia's artisan past thanks to its independent fashion designers

Peering into the windows of the little Gràcia craft and clothing ateliers is an insight into the neighbourhood's manufacturing past. As you stroll its shaded streets, you will stumble upon whimsical boutiques and pop-up studios where people are putting their heart and soul into recovering the quality of traditional design, albeit using modern materials.

One of the growing bunch of Gràcia's young grassroots fashion creators is Helena García, who runs the small **Ven Y Cogelo** (Caller Ramón y Cajal, 6; map E1). Describing herself as a *ropa de autor* (a 'cloth artisan'), she sits at the back of her studio shop sewing away to produce her colourful garments – viscose dresses and miniskirts, fleece vests and sweaters in cheerful and fun prints. Her decorative arts background in painting and printing comes through the graphic colours and textures, some classic, others she concedes downright crazy with their prints and waves. The store also curates items from other designers including jewellery and accessories.

Men are not forgotten and should head to **José Rivero** (Carrer d'Astúries, 43; map E2) for white Bermudas and print shirts. In his shop – all brick and wood beam –

he also sells a women's collection of cotton sundresses in classical or breezy patterned prints, and satin evening dresses.

Closer to the Avinguda Diagonal, is the swish emporium of **Lydia Delgado** (Carrer de Séneca, 28; map E1), a far more established designer working with traditional tailoring techniques whose tagline is 'the bohemian side of elegance'. Collaborating with her daughter, the 'Miranda for Lydia' line combines mum's palette of bright pink and attention-grabbing colours, with an eccentric edge and references to Japan and Los Angeles.

Get a taste of Gràcia's green lifestyle

Gràcia is a very down-to-earth neighbourhood with a strong green, eco-friendly ethos. This is especially visible to the tourist in its myriad eco fashion and organic food shops.

Proving that green and design can go together is **GreenLifeStyle** (Torrent de l'Olla, 95; map E1), where clothes, bags and footwear are displayed among more vintage props such as retro TV sets and cash registers, all against crisp white walls.

In sourcing brands, owner Carolina's manifesto is a firm commitment to sustainability, recycling and fair trade plus strong design aesthetics. All clothes sold here are made in Europe, including leggings from Barcelona designer Bloi, heavenly soft organic cotton tops from French brand Les Racines du Ciel, trousers and vests from Austrian label MILCH, which upcycles men's suits into women's clothing, and German-based caro e., whose poetic handcrafted designs are spun from high-quality natural yarns like alpaca, cashmere and merino.

At **SoleRebels** (Carrer d'Astúries, 47; map E2), which has a sprinkling of stores worldwide, the shoes are handmade in Ethiopia by artisans using recycled tire soles and organic fabrics.

And if you feel like an organic snack at any point during your eco-shopping, duck into **Biopassió** (Plaça de la Vila de Gràcia, 11; map E1), where you'll find honey, herbs, fruit and nuts, bonbons and biscuits, oils and ointments all packaged up enticingly and beautifully presented. They also make for the perfect savoury gift or souvenir.

Have a ball at one of Gràcia's street festivals

Nearly every day is a festival in Gràcia but watch out for the folkloric festivals which animate every tiny alleyway of this laid-back but vibrant neighbourhood. Don't hesitate to join in, as it's a great way to get to know the real Gràcia and its residents. Children, especially, will delight in the fun and colourful street life.

If you have a sweet tooth don't miss out on the **Fiesta de Sant Medir**, usually on the first Saturday of March, during which brightly wrapped *caramelos* (sweets, not just toffees) are thrown with gay abandon around the streets and delivered to all the participating shops which put them in baskets up front. The *collas* (revellers) parade through the neighbourhood giving out sweets to all those who attend.

Gràcia's largely care-free network of streets makes it ideal for street parties. For **La Festa Major de Gràcia**, a week-long festival around mid-August, decorating competitions transform the streets into works of art, and there are concerts at bandstands in the main squares and street stalls galore. Everyone has a wild time.

Barcelona's most important traditional festival is the legendary **Colles de Geganters de Catalunya**, which sees costumed giants and children's *colles de diables* (little devils) amongst other characters parade through the neighbourhood.

You'll see the same kinds of processions during **La Mercè**, a *festa* honouring the city's patron saint that takes place throughout the city over five days in late September but which Gràcia takes part in with its typical gutsy zest. This is when the **Castellers de Vila de Gràcia**, the shoulder-upon-shoulder human castles, try to give the 33.5m (110ft)-tall clock tower in the Plaça de la Vila de Gràcia a run for its money. The Human Towers of Catalonia are so unique and spectacular that they made it onto Unesco's World Heritage list.

Catch a film or an opera at Gràcia's arthouse Cines Verdi

Find respite from the heat, or from sightseeing, by watching a VOSE original version film (with Spanish subtitles).

A fixture of Gràcia's urban village culture, **Cines Verdi** is one of Barcelona's leading independent cinemas with a varied programme of art-house, experimental and new release films, mostly European but also Asian and American.

The five-screen Verdi actually spills over into the four-screen **Cinemes Verdi Park** round the corner.

There are also live screenings of operas and ballets from leading opera houses including Paris's Opéra Garnier and London's Royal Opera House, while Verdi Kids has a fun programme of short and full-length animation films for little ones – some in original version.

Cinephiles also keep a watch out for various film festivals including **La Fiesta del cine!** in May.

Cines Verdi; Carrer de Verdi, 32; screening times generally 10am–10.30pm; tel 93 238 7990; www.cines-verdi.com; map F2

Enjoy the best free view in Barcelona from Park Güell

After climbing up the hill or taking the elevator to **Park Güell**, enter the free area of the park from the steep Avinguda del Coll del Portell bordering its southern side, giving access to gorgeous tropical gardens and spectacular views.

The so-called Monumental Zone was cordoned off in 2013 to protect the most vulnerable, heavily visited part of the park, where all the Gaudí gems are located. But this zone, which is ticketed, occupies just under 8 percent of the entire park.

When the industrialist Eusebi Güell commissioned Gaudí in 1901 to design a suburban 'garden city' for well-to-do families in this wooded area, he set up a complex network of paths, viaducts and steps to deal with the convoluted terrain. Of the original 60 houses planned, only 5 were completed.

Follow the winding stone path through lush garden beds until you reach the lookout point, a small stone citadel topped with three crosses, called the 'Calvari'. It sits on the park's highest point, the 182m (597ft) **Turó de les Tres Creus** (Hill of the Three Crosses), from which there are sweeping views, across the neighbouring Parc del Carmel to the Pedralbes Monastery all the way to the sea.

Take the eastern stairway down to Carrer de l'Olot to continue to the Monumental Zone. From the top of the steep railing, there is a bird's eye view over the fantasyland of coloured baubles and icing-like decoration of the park's squares, houses and pillars. From out front, before the monumental gatehouse, it looks like a giant gingerbread house ... with the addition of the ceramic dragon.

Park Güell, Monumental Zone (buy your tickets at www.parkguell.cat/en); autumn–winter 8.30am–6pm, spring–summer 8am–9.30pm; map F3

Hit the Gaudí trail through Gràcia

Gràcia was Gaudí's home patch for nearly two decades from 1906 until 1925. In his day, as he walked from his Park Güell residence to the Sagrada Família, Gràcia would have actually been a village – reached from Barcelona through a track of open fields.

Gaudí lived in one of the two houses built on the Güell estate, designed by his friend and close collaborator Francesc d'Assís Berenguer i Mestres. Constructed as a show home for the Park Güell residential project, in 1963 it became the **Casa Museu Gaudí**. Nestled in lush gardens in the northwest corner of the park, the flamingo-pink house is also a showcase for his imaginative furniture designs.

Gaudí's first major commission, in 1888, was **Casa Vicens**. A private home then as it is now, it's a lovely 2km (1.2 miles) walk down the hilly streets of Gràcia to reach it. Though not open to visitors, the exteriors of Moorish- and oriental-inspired green and white tiles are worth the walk. It'll give you a glimpse into Gaudí's characteristic design process, using nature as his muse. He made the plant motifs for the cast-iron railings from clay models of the fan palm, and drew inspiration from the French marigolds growing in his garden to design the pressed tiles.

Not coincidentally, Manuel Vicens Montaner, who commissioned the building, was a tile manufacturer. The house's myriad coloured ceramic tiles and turrets are reminiscent of Mudejar, Indian and Japanese art forms and this exotisism was greeted far more enthusiastically by the Barcelona elite than Gaudí's later landmarks such as the Casa Milà–La Pedrera.

*Casa Museu Gaudí, Park Güell; Carretera del Carmel, 23A; not included in the Park Güell ticket; Apr–Sept 9am–8pm, 10am–6pm Oct–Mar; www.casamuseugaudi.org; map F3
Casa Vicens; Carrer de les Carolines, 18–24; map E2*

Soak up the sun in the Plaça del Sol

It's not hard to see how the **Plaça del Sol** got its name. A sun-soaked peaceful haven by day, a lively hub by night, it's also one of the best places to soak up Gràcia's bohemian airs and spirited local life on a cosy scale.

What is hard to believe is that there was a bomb shelter here during the Civil War, which was later turned into a public toilet, thankfully demolished in 1986 during the city's era of urban renewal.

The astronomy buffs who urbanised the square in the 1840s also named the surrounding streets Carrer de la Planeta, del Sol, de la Lluna (Catalan spelling of moon), Minerva, Neptú, Venus, Eclipse, Star, etc. though only the first six survive.

The astrological theme continues in recent additions such as the **Astrolabi**, a bronze sundial sculpture by Joaquim Camps on one side of the square.

Contemporary architects also designed the sun-setting streetlamps, symmetrical garden beds, stone benches and the rectangular gazebo, which is a bandstand for regular music and festivals – though you might prefer to join the young people who opt to sit on the ground.

On the northern side of the quadrant, a cluster of picturesque

tin soldier-tall houses add a bit of flounce, painted in pastel shades with miniature balconies and fancy cornices.

One of them, a remarkable peppermint-green and pink Modernista house with seashell-like windows on the corner (13) is home to one of the squares many cafés and restaurants, **Envalira**. This family-run place specialises in rice dishes – it's Spanish cooking at its most genuine.

Another great option is **Sol Soler** (21), which serves delicious alternative tapas, with plenty of vegetarian options.

Plaça del Sol; map E1

Join in the *vermut* hour in Gràcia

In Barcelona *vermut* is a source of home-grown pride, given that Spain's most traditional tipple comes from Reus on the Catalan coast.

More aromatic than its Italian and French equivalents, due to the quantity of botanicals packed in Spanish vermouth: herbs, fruits, roots and spices, it's then macerated in alcohol and water, mixed with wine, and at times, barrel-aged.

The *hora del vermut* is a regional hymn, generally starting from mid-afternoon it goes on, and on... The bars of Gràcia will tell you in name alone how much the vermouth hour tradition endures – and how trendy it has actually become. Cue **La Vermu** (Carrer de Sant Domènec, 15; Mon–Thu 6.30pm–midnight, Fri–Sat 12.30–4pm & 6.30pm–midnight, Sun 12.30–4pm;

map E1), one of the trendier and most recent additions to the *vermut* scene already has a faithful following of aficionados.

Just a hole in the wall, it looks like a British Royal Mailbox from the outside with its red iron shutters. Inside people clink little glasses of the dark red-brown liquor at a sprinkling of bar seats and tables. As always various varieties are served here including a home brew, and a less bitter white *vermut*. Soak it up with some tapas: stuffed olives, marinated sardines, smoked salmon, anchovies and mussels are some of the stand-out ones here.

La Vermutería del Tano (Bruniquer, 30; Mon–Fri 9am–9pm, Sat–Sun noon–4pm; map F1) on the other hand is an old-timer vermouth cellar, with casks and a clock collection lining the walls. It's not chic but it's authentic.

Another buzzing youthful place to try is **Café Salambó** (Carrer de Torrijos, 51; Mon–Thu noon–1am, Fri–Sat until 3am, Sun noon–midnight; www.cafesalambo.com; map F2), a lofty theatre-like space with designer lighting, wooden furnishings, a billiards table, wine barrels everywhere and attractively-priced menus.

Eat with the locals in La Vila de Gràcia

La Vila de Gràcia is the historic centre of old Gràcia. Radiating out from the main town square Plaça de la Vila de Gràcia, and swept in by the neighbourhood's three main axes – Gran de Gràcia, Torrent de l'Olla and Travessera de Gràcia – the independent village atmosphere thrives here.

In the **Plaça de la Vila de Gràcia** (map E1) it's immediately clear that this is a close-knit community – from the buzzing café-bars where crowds gather from early morning, to the groups of elderly residents chewing the fat under the fig trees.

Take a seat under the towering 1864-built clock tower, or join the locals for breakfast coffee and pastries at the bright art-decked **Nabucco Tiramisu** (8). If it's lunchtime consider **Amélie Restaurante** (11), loved for its fajitas, risotto, burgers and hearty bowls of vegetable soups. Or quench your thirst next door at **Cadaqués** (11) which also does seafood. The terraces of all three form a little sea of alfresco seats on the square.

For food to go, **Piano Piano** (7) do tasty organic *piadina* and pizza, and hole-in-the-wall **Kakigori** (3) serves up Japanese *dorayaki* pancakes, from traditional red-bean to salmon or even Nutella.

Continue your village jaunt by walking to the **Mercat de la Llibertat** (Plaça de la Llibertat, 27; map E1) a Modernista market built in 1888 where farmers from the hills above used to come to sell their produce.

SANTS AND MONTJUÏC

Montjuïc

Ⓔ

0   100   200   300   400   500 m

0   100   200   300   400   500 yds

Ⓓ

Ⓒ

Gran Via de les Corts Catalanes

Carrer   de   Sant   Fructuós

C. de Traia

Carrer del Polvorí

Av. de Francesc Ferrer i Guàrdia

CaixaForum

Plaça
de Sant
Jordi

Poble
Espanyol

Barcelo
Pavil

Av. dels Montanyans

Palau
Victòr
Eugèn

C. Jocs del 92

Pl.
Hidràulica

Avinguda

Passeig

INEFC
Universitat
de l'Esport

Plaça
d'Europa

Palau Naci
Ò
Museu Nacional
d'Art de
Catalunya

Piscines
Bernat
Picornell

Camp de
Beisbol

JARDINS
JOAN
MARAGALL

de

Plaça del Mig
de Can Clos

C. de la Pedrera del Mussol

C. Jocs del 92

Torre de
Calatrava

Carrer Jocs del 92

l'Estadi

C. de Can Clos

ANELLA
OLÍMPICA

Palau
Sant Jordi

Complex Esportiu
La Bàscula

Estadi
Olímpic

C. dels Ferrocarrils Catalans

Carrer del Foc

Passeig Olímpic

PARC DE MONTJUÏC

C. Doctor i Font Q

Passeig del Midgia

FOSSAR DE LA
PEDRERA

PARC DEL MIGDIA

JARDÍ
BOTÀNIC

CEMENTIRI
DEL SUD-OEST

Passeig   del   Migdia

CEMENTIRI DE MONTJUÏC

Ⓐ   Ⓑ   Ⓒ   Ⓓ

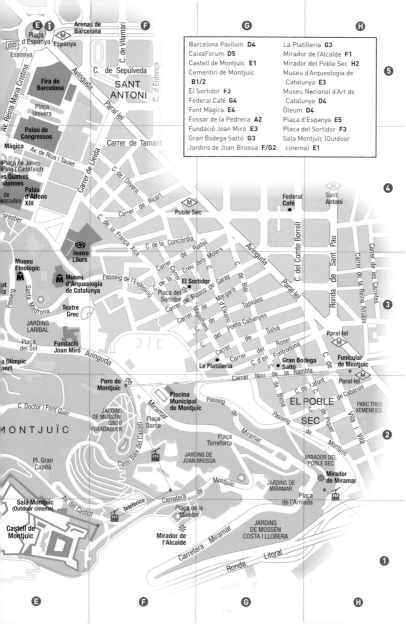

Barcelona Pavilion **D4**
CaixaForum **D5**
Castell de Montjuïc **E1**
Cementiri de Montjuïc **B1/2**
El Sortidor **F3**
Federal Café **G4**
Font Màgica **E4**
Fossar de la Pedrera **A2**
Fundació Joan Miró **E3**
Gran Bodega Saltó **G3**
Jardins de Joan Brossa **F/G2**

La Platilleria **G3**
Mirador de l'Alcalde **F1**
Mirador del Poble Sec **H2**
Museu d'Arqueologia de Catalunya **E3**
Museu Nacional d'Art de Catalunya **D4**
Òleum **D4**
Plaça d'Espanya **E5**
Plaça del Sortidor **F3**
Sala Montjuïc (Outdoor cinema) **E1**

Hang out in hilly, multicultural El Poble Sec and dig into Catalonia's archaeological past

Nestled into the foothills of Montjuïc, El Poble Sec is one of Barcelona's most distinctive villages. There is a different pace here among its sloping streets, wedged between the greenery of the **Mirador del Poble Sec** (Paseo de Montjuïc, 28; map H2) park and lookout just above – which offers a stunning night-time view – and the belting stretch of Avinguda del Parallel.

What it lacks in tourist attractions it makes up with convivial atmosphere, and bar-restaurants here are a mix of Argentinian, Italian, Catalan and Galician.

At **La Platilleria** (Carrer del Roser, 82; tel 934 635 401; map G3), in the upper heights of Poble Sec, sit at the bar by the piano, among vintage props, and enjoy a *vermutito* from the vermouth menu or a *birrita* from the beer menu. The tapas are traditional little dishes (*platillos*) of fish, potato, cheese and sausage.

Pork dishes, *patatas bravas* and pasta on a pretty square, are all on offer at **El Sortidor** (Plaça del Sortidor, 5; map F3), a timepiece with its white marble tables set against a sweep of pastel stained-glass windows.

For a bar with a story to tell, traditional tapas and live music, head to the **Gran Bodega Saltó** (Carrer de Blesa, 36; tel: 934 413 709; map G3). The interior of wine barrels, vintage *porrones* (wine pitchers) and stuffed tigers looks a bit like a buccaneer's den. Back in the 1920s, it was a wholesale wine cellar and store, where housewives would look for wine in bulk, a chat and a show. Locals are still known to drop by at night to fill up their wine jugs directly from the barrels. And music is still very important here, with flamenco, jazz, blues and folk sessions. On Sunday afternoons, in keeping with Barcelona tradition, it holds a 'Vermut Musical'.

Somehow the **Museu d'Arqueologia de Catalunya** (Passeig de Santa Madrona, 39–41, tel: 934 23 21 49; Tue–Sat 9.30am–7pm, Sun 10am–2.30pm; www.mac.cat; map E3) fits perfectly with El Poble Sec's eclecticism. Although the information is in Catalan only, it is a great insight into the lives of the first Catalonians.

Be dazzled by the all-singing, all-dancing magic Montjuïc fountain

It delighted revellers at the 1929 International Exhibition and the **Font Màgica de Montjuïc** (Plaça de Carles Buïgas, 1) continues to do so with its *son et lumière* shows of colour-changing water acrobatics set to music (April to October) – a liquid ballet sustained by recycled water.

Designed by engineer Carles Buïgas, this imposing ornamental fountain is truly majestic by night, set against the golden silhouette of the Palau Nacional, and the illuminated Avinguda de la Reina Maria Cristina rolled up to it like a red carpet.

This is also where the Piromusical is held, the *son et lumière* capping off Barcelona's main festival, La Mercè in September. The grand finale takes on an international flavour, and in 2016 it paid homage to two departed music legends, David Bowie and Prince.

The views from the square are impressive too, stretching across the ceremonial Plaça d'Espanya nearby to mount Tibidabo, the highest peak above the city at 550m (1,804ft).

Some 500m/yards away, the **Plaça d'Espanya** (map E5) has its very own monumental fountain, an allegorical mass of marble, wrought-iron and bronze by Gaudí associate Josep Maria Jujol. Its sculptures are a nod to the three bodies of water surrounding the Iberian Peninsula – the Mediterranean, the Atlantic and the Bay of Biscay – and to the main rivers running through it – the Ebre, the Tagus and the Guadalquivir. The imposing 33m (108ft)-high cascade is a welcoming sight for travellers arriving to the city from Barcelona Sants train station close by.

Font Màgica de Montjuïc; shows every half hour Apr–May, Sept–Oct Sat 9–10.30pm, Jun–Aug Thu–Sun 9.30–11pm; map E4

Seek refuge in a former amusement park that's still a crowd-pleaser

A former amusement park, Montjuïc's **Jardins de Joan Brossa** is a wonderful leafy retreat on hot summer days, with bars, picnic tables and restaurants all in close range.

With its lofty views, smattering of poetry excerpts and sculptures, this little oasis was named after a Catalan poet, as are many of Montjuïc's gardens. Brossa's poem, *Música d'Arpa*, graces a plaque at the main entrance.

Part woodland, part city garden, among the carpet of perennials, the conifers, cedars, pines and cypresses are many exotic species – Atlas, Himalayan and Lebanon cedars, Arizona and Monterey cypresses, ornamental pagoda trees and acacias.

The fun park atmosphere still lingers and little ones will enjoy the playgrounds, zip lines and climbing frames. One path through the park has 'musical cushions', which emit sounds when you step on them – a sure hit with the littlest ones.

Quirky relics have been recycled from the old park, including the old Fanta Bar – a strange brutalist concrete structure shaped like a large sunshade, thus nicknamed *parasol*.

Jardins de Joan Brossa; Plaça Dante; map F/G2

Go up, up in a cable car and away to a castle

If you want to take the shortcut to the Montjuïc Castle, or just go for an exhilarating ride, head to the Parc de Montjuïc to hop on the **Telefèric de Montjuïc** cable car to the top of the hill (cabins seat up to 8 people).

As you glide over the treetops of Montjuïc's extensive parklands the panoramas progressively open up and sweep over city, port, sea and mountain chains in the far distance.

The ride stops just a couple of hundred metres/yards short of the **Castell de Montjuïc** whose fortressed hulk has dominated the port from 173m (567ft) above since 1640.

You can walk along its walls and in the landscaped grounds, re-stored in the mid-18th century after suffering extensive damage during the War of the Spanish Succession, when it was a key defence point.

This is very much a castle that children will enjoy. Add a cable-car ride and you have a winning combo.

Stretch out the views by walking back down.

Castell de Montjuïc; Carretera de Montjuïc, 66; daily Oct–Mar 10am–6pm, Apr–Sept 10am–8pm; map E1

Get a culture fix in an old Modernista textile factory

Barcelona has a very big bevy of bold, modernist constructions. The **CaixaForum** illustrates the way Catalan art nouveau, or Modernisme, architecture stemmed from the city's industrial boom of the early 1900s.

The old Casaramona textile factory was designed by Josep Puig i Cadafalch in 1911, and was later turned into an exhibition centre named after the bank that bought it.

The grand rectangular brick and iron complex inspired by medieval castles comprises 11 variously shaped buildings connected with cast-iron columns and surmounted by a sweep of pinnacles.

The entrance is striking with its contemporary steel and glass canopy in the shape of a tree, a work by Japanese architect Arata Isozaki.

Inside, a wonderful space plays host to a turnover of quality exhibitions on art, cinema, photography and multimedia. There is also a guided tour, Modernisme-Modernity, that's well worth joining.

And even if you don't take in any exhibition, entry is free to the white-marble rooftop terrace, where the café overlooks the National Palace.

CaixaForum; Avinguda Ferrer i Guàrdia, 6–8; tel: 934 768 600; www.laCaixa.es; daily 10am–8pm, Jul–Aug Wed until 11pm; map D5

Tread the turf of the city's beloved Barça club or attend a match at Europe's largest stadium

Matching La Rambla for crowds, the **Camp Nou** stadium, home to the illustrious FC Barcelona football club since 1957, was originally supposed to be called 'Estadi del FC Barcelo'. But fans took to calling it 'Camp Nou' – the 'new ground' – as it was replacing the club's old home at Les Corts, and the more familiar name stuck.

The largely concrete and iron stadium was designed by architects Francesc Mitjans Miró and Josep Soteras Mauri, at a price tag which left the club seriously indebted for years.

Packing nearly 100,000 spectators into the stadium has helped pay that off. Five Olympic swimming pools in length and over four in width, and nearly one at its maximum height, it cannot fail to impress.

The self-guided tours of the Camp Nou take in the stands, the pitch and team dugout, the players' tunnel and dressing room, press room, com-mentary boxes and a multimedia museum with a most impressive trophy gallery. And Messi fans rest assured, there is a lot of fuss around the club's star player, winner of an incredible 5 ballons d'or (and counting).

To get the full experience, try and attend a La Liga game, the Spanish premier league. The atmosphere is out of this world, whether you are level with the players or all the way up.

But be quick, the Camp Nou is about to become the 'new Camp Nou' as a cosmetic transformation goes under way during the 2017/18 season to increase the capacity to 105,000 and is planned to be completed in the 2020/21 campaign. There will be no disruption to the matches.

Camp Nou; Carrer d'Aristides Maillol; daily 9.30am–3.30pm, 5 or 8.45pm but times vary according to match calendar so check website; www.fcbarcelona.com

Climb up Montjuïc for a Mayor's View of the city

Start with the gardened way along the Passeig de Josep Carner, skirting the Jardins de Walter Benjamin, where you will be tracing the Montjuïc sports circuit – a jogger's delight. Information panels point out the various itineraries and distances involved.

Next, from the Passeig de Montjuïc you'll follow a gentle winding path up to the tiered **Jardins del Mirador de l'Alcalde** (Carretera de Montjuïc, 41; map F1) whose 'Mayor's Viewing Point' offers some of the city's best panoramas over land and sea.

The intriguing disc-shaped mosaic paving the viewpoint, designed by Catalan artist Joan Josep Tharrats in the 1960s, is made from a Gaudiesque variety of materials: pebbles, paving stones, bricks, tiles, broken fragments of glass and concrete and iron chains, cogs, filaments, screws and bolts.

While there is a cable car to the top of Barcelona's mythical mountain and castle (see page 155), the climb is relatively easy and very rewarding.

From the Plaça de les Drassanes near the shipyard and the Columbus Monument, you have a breezy 2.5km (1.5 miles), or 35-minute walk thereabouts to the lookout at the top, though it is much more enjoyable done over a couple of hours taking in all the stops, primarily gardens, along the way.

Continue your ascend amongst the Aleppo pines, dwarf palms, Canary Island palms and huge sago palms past lovely statues and an ornamental fountain.

If you do want to continue on to the Montjuïc Castle (see page 155) by foot you have only about 500m/ yards to go.

Admire Miró's colourful work in his striking museum

Born in Barcelona in 1893, Joan Miró's art was far more influenced by his years spent abroad, rubbing shoulders with the Surrealist poets in Paris and the Abstract Expressionists in New York in the 1940s. He was also very attached to the small Catalan town of Mont-roig del Camp where he summered, and his refuge on the island of Mallorca.

To house his body of works, the **Fundació Joan Miró** was established and designed by his close friend, the architect and city planner Josep Lluís Sert, in 1975. An exponent of avant-garde architecture in Catalonia, the result was a bright white cube rising up five levels and crowned with roof lanterns.

Hailed as a 'rationalist landmark', the Spanish modernist equivalent of German Bauhaus or French Le Corbusier purism, the gallery combines a precise, orderly design with a Mediterranean-style central courtyard, roof terrace and skylights.

These all allow light to pour into the galleries, which one of the largest collection of Miró's work: his complete graphic work but also paintings, drawings and sculptures arranged thematically according to the artist's typically unconventional, cerebral ethos, 'Beyond Painting', 'Escape', 'Anonymity' and 'Anti-Painting'.

Highlights include his Surrealist paintings on the Spanish Civil War, and the renowned large canvases of big bright brush strokes, produced in his later life. Then you can head outside, walk through the gardens among his sculptures or go up to the roof, and take in the incredible views, as art, architecture and landscape blend into one.

Fundació Joan Miró; Parc de Montjuïc; tel: 934 439 470; www.fmirobcn.org; Nov–Mar Tue, Wed, Fri 10am–6pm, Apr–Oct 10am–8pm, Thur 10am–9pm, Sat 10am–8pm, Sun 10am–3pm; map E3

Grasp Barcelona's gruesome past at Montjuïc's mass grave

Tucked away in a corner of the Montjuïc Cemetery, the **Fossar de la Pedrera** was used as a mass grave for 4,000 victims of Franco's White Terror from 1939 onwards.

Most were Republicans accused of 'military rebellion' and executed by Franco's repressive regime at their preferred killing ground, the Camp de la Bota – today's Fòrum – then their bodies brought back here, dumped and covered with quicklime.

In 1985 the abandoned quarry was transformed into a moving memorial for the victims of the Civil War, after years of campaigning by the families.

A highly evocative, peaceful place, set deep on verdant lawns within the quarry's high sandstone walls, as you walk up into the Fossar, you will pass a series of tributes chiselled in concrete. There

are other memorials here, notably one to the victims of Nazism.

One of the most famous graves here belongs to Republican hero and Catalan President Lluís Companys, executed at Montjuïc Castle by the Francoist regime in October 1940.

Fossar de la Pedrera; Carrer de la Mare de Déu de Port, 56–66; map A2

Civil War Tours

Off the beaten path, consider joining Spanish Civil War Tours in Barcelona (info@spanishcivilwartours.com) which include this little-known mass grave on their itineraries. Much loved by historians, activists and journalists, the company is part run by British-born and Barcelona-based Nick Lloyd, author of the guide *Forgotten Places: Barcelona and the Spanish Civil War*.

Marvel at Mies van der Rohe's iconic Barcelona Pavilion

High on the Montjuïc hill stands the **Barcelona Pavilion**, a shimmering rectangular pavilion of smooth proportions, all marble and glass and slender steel columns.

Built by Ludwig Mies van der Rohe as the German Pavilion for the 1929 Exhibition – a showcase for the Weimar Republic who commissioned it to promote a modern progressive Germany – it was later dismantled, but, at the instigation of some leading architects, rebuilt in 1986 to celebrate the centenary of the architect's birth.

Its clean lines are quite breathtaking, and clarify the significance and beauty of minimalism. A blend of four shades of tinted glass, with marble, onyx, chromed steel and travertine, it is beautifully reflected in the flat-pebbled pools.

This minimalist gem is a favourite amongst the architects and fashion designers who adhere by van der Rohe's exemplary sleek, rational architecture – 'less is more' as he once famously said.

Barcelona Pavilion; Avinguda Francesc Ferrer i Guàrdia, 7; tel: 932 151 011; Mar–Oct Mon–Sun 10am–8pm, Nov–Feb 10am–6pm; www.miesbcn.com; map D4

Soak up Catalan art history and 360-degree views

Join culture vultures at the **Museu Nacional d'Art de Catalunya** housed in the Palau Nacional, dramatically fronted by an impressive multi-tiered water cascade.

The cavernous **Palau Nacional** was erected for the 1929 Exhibition as host centre, and its great dome was inspired by the one in St Peter's in Rome and its two lesser domes on each side and four towers by the Cathedral of Santiago de Compostela.

Gothic, modernism, Renaissance and Baroque – all the great epochs of Catalan and international art are represented in its soft-lit rooms. It also houses the greatest collection of Romanesque art in Europe, including many murals transported from the apses of historic Catalan churches. Dating from the 11th to the 13th centuries, these paintings, along with altarscreens, chests, madonnas and crucifixes, are brightly coloured and executed with a powerful simplicity that has inspired many modern Catalan painters.

The Throne Room, with the balcony from where King Alfonso XIII inaugurated the world fair, now houses the restaurant **Òleum** where two-star chef Fina Puigdevall serves up truffle risottos and other Mediterranean delights.

End your visit by going up to the Rooftop Viewpoint cocktail bar, or to the separate rooftop terrace to enjoy wonderful 360-degree views sweeping in the Sagrada Família, the Torre Agbar and Vila Olímpica seafront.

Museu Nacional d'Art de Catalunya (MNAC); Palau Nacional; Parc de Montjuïc; tel: 936 220 376; May–Sept Tue–Sat 10am–8pm, Oct–Apr 10am–6pm, Sun year-round 10am–3pm; free Sat from 3pm and first Sun of every month; www.museunacional.cat; map D4 Òleum; Tue–Sun 12.30–4pm; tel: 932 890 679; www.oleum-barcelona.com

Take in a film under the stars at Montjuïc Castle

Barcelona loves its outdoor cinemas and during the summer, there's no better place to be than up in Montjuïc Castle, which turns into a fantastic outdoor cinema and concert venue for the **Sala Montjuïc**, a month-long programme of film classics and new releases. All films are screened in English with Spanish subtitles.

The late-night movies kick off with live music performances, from bossa nova and flamenco to R&B and traditional Portuguese fado vocals, or with a short film.

The breezy evenings and glowing views over the city provide a haven from the heat in the city below. Bring a well-stocked picnic from your favourite Barcelona deli, and a blanket, or alternatively you can rent lounge chairs on the spot. Then settle on the lawns with the convivial sing-along crowd and get ready for a night at the movies under the stars.

Sala Montjuïc; Montjuïc Castle Gardens; tel 933 023 553; see website for exact dates www.salamontjuic.org, screenings Mon, Wed and Fri at 10pm, concerts start at 8.45pm; map E1

163

ESSENTIALS

ADMISSION CHARGES

Most museums have an entry charge, with the usual reductions for children, students and the over-65s. The Articket (€30) allows entry to Barcelona's six main museums for three months (www.articketbcn.org). The Arqueoticket (from €13.50) provides entry to four museums with archaeological collections and is valid for a year. Discounts apply when you buy online at www.barcelonaturisme.com. Buy the Modernisme Route (www.rutadel modernisme.com) guidebook, available in bookshops across the city, to get discounts of up to 50 percent off entry fees to all Modernista monuments in the city. A combined Barcelona Card offers free entry or substantial discounts at Barcelona's most important museums as well as free travel on public transport. A three-day card costs €40.50. Many Barcelona museums offer free admission on Sunday afternoons from 3–8pm and free admission for the whole day on the first Sunday of every month.

CLIMATE

Barcelona's mild Mediterranean climate assures sunshine most of the year and freezing temperatures are rare, even in winter. Spring and autumn are the most agreeable seasons. Midsummer can be hot and humid; at times a thick mist hangs over the city. Average temperatures in winter are 10°C (54°F) and 25°C (75°F) in summer. Nov and Feb–Mar are the wettest months.

CRIME AND SAFETY

Be on your guard against pickpockets and bag snatchers (be wary of people offering 'assistance' or becoming suddenly interested in you), especially in the Rambla and Old Town, and at major tourist sights. Try to avoid deserted alleyways. Do not leave luggage unattended; do not carry more money than you need; make use of the hotel safe; do not leave valuables on view in a car. The blue-clad, mobile anti-crime squads are out in force on the Rambla and principal thoroughfares. Should you be a crime victim, make a report (denuncia) at the nearest police station (comisaría) – vital for insurance claims. The main one in the Old Town is at Nou de la Rambla, 76–78, or call the Mossos d'Esquadra (112). You can also report theft at most city hotels.

CUSTOMS

Free exchange of non-duty-free items for personal use is permitted between Spain and other EU countries (800 cigarettes, limited amounts of alcohol and perfume). Visitors may bring up to €10,000 into or out of Spain without a declaration. If you intend to bring in or out larger sums, declare this on arrival and departure.

D

DISABLED TRAVELLERS

The city has many hotels with facilities (see www.barcelona-access.com, or check with the tourist office). Many museums and historic buildings are wheelchair-accessible. The beaches have suitable access, and there are many adapted public toilets. Some bus and nearly all metro stations have facilities for disabled travellers (see www.tmb.cat/en/transport-accessible). For adapted taxi information, call tel: 93 420 80 88.

For further information contact the Institut Municipal de Persones amb Discapacitat (Carrer de València, 344, 08013 Barcelona; tel: 93 413 27 75; Mon–Fri 9am–2pm).

E

ELECTRICITY

The standard is 220 volts, but some hotels have 110–120 in the bathrooms as a safety precaution. Check before plugging in any of your appliances.

Power sockets take round, two-pin plugs, so British visitors will need an international adapter. US visitors will also need a transformer, unless they have dual-voltage travel appliances.

EMBASSIES AND CONSULATES

Most Western European countries have consulates in Barcelona. All the embassies are in Madrid.
Canada: Plaça de Catalunya, 9; tel: 93 412 72 36.
Ireland: Gran Vía Carles III, 94; tel: 93 491 50 21.

UK: Avinguda Diagonal 477, 13; tel: 93 366 6200.
US: Passeig de la Reina Elisenda de Montcada, 23; tel: 93 280 22 27.

EMERGENCIES

General emergencies: 112
Mossos d'Esquadra (Autonomous Catalan Police): 112
Municipal (city) police: 092
Fire: 080

G

GAY AND LESBIAN TRAVELLERS

Barcelona has an active gay community and scores of clubs and nightlife options. Conservative Catholic beliefs still predominate in some sectors, so gay visitors may wish to be discreet. The gay and lesbian hotline is 900 601 601. The free magazine *Nois* has information and listings of clubs, restaurants and other entertainment options (for download). Casal Lambda is a gay cultural centre (Carrer de Verdaguer i Callis, 10; tel: 93 319 55 50; www.lambda.cat; open from 5pm).

The nearby town of Sitges, just half an hour south of the city on the coast, is a real magnet for gay people, particularly in summer, and is well worth a visit.

H

HEALTH

Standards of hygiene are high, and medical care is generally excellent; most doctors speak sufficient English.

It is wise to ease yourself into the climate and food gently. In summer, is it advisable to wear a hat and sun-cream during the day. You should also avoid any tired-looking tapas during the hotter months. The water is safe to drink, but can have a strong taste; bottled water is inexpensive.

EU citizens with corresponding health insurance facilities are entitled to medical and hospital treatment under the Spanish social security system – you need a **European Health Insurance Card**, obtainable from post offices or online.

In an emergency, go to the *Urgencias* department of a main hospital:
Hospital de la Santa Creu i Sant Pau: Sant Quintí, 89; tel: 93 556 5775; www.santpau.cat.
Hospital Clinic de Barcelona: Villarroel, 170; tel: 93 227 54 00; www.hospitalclinic.org.
Hospital de Sant Joan de Déu: Passeig Sant Joan de Déu, 2; tel: 93 600 97 83.

For an ambulance, go to an *ambulatorio* (medical centre) or call 061.

Pharmacies *(farmàcia)* operate as a first line of defence, as pharmacists can prescribe drugs and are usually adept at making on-the-spot diagnoses. There is always one in each district that stays open all night and on public holidays.

HOLIDAYS

Many bars, restaurants and museums close in the afternoon and evening on public holidays and Sundays. August is the annual holiday month, and many businesses, including restaurants, may close down for three or four weeks.

1 Jan: *Año Nuevo* (New Year's Day)
6 Jan: *Epifanía* (Epiphany)
1 May: *Fiesta de Trabajo* (Labour Day)
24 June: *San Juan* (St John's Day)
15 Aug: *Asunción* (Assumption)
11 Sept: *La Diada* (Catalan National Day)
24 Sept: *La Mercè* (Day of Mercedes, Barcelona's patron saint)
1 Nov: *Todos los Santos* (All Saints' Day)
6 Dec: *Día de la Constitución* (Constitution Day)
8 Dec: *Inmaculada Concepció* (Immaculate Conception)
25–26 Dec: *Navidad* (Christmas)
Movable Feasts:
Feb/Mar: *Mardi Gras* (Shrove Tuesday/ Carnival)
Late Mar/Apr: *Viernes Santo* (Good Friday)
Late Mar/Apr: *Lunes de Pascua* (Easter Monday)
Early to mid-June: *Corpus Christi* (Corpus Christi)

I

INTERNET

There are numerous places where internet access is cheap and easy. The city council provides a free Wi-Fi network, covering nearly 600 hotspots across the city, mostly at municipal buildings (Mon–Sun 8am–1am). See the map to find the nearest one at www.bcn.cat/ barcelonawifi/en/. A few old-fashioned Internet cafés still operate in Barcelona.

L

LEFT LUGGAGE

Left-luggage lockers *(consigna)* are available in the main railway stations (Sants and Estació de França), at Barcelona Nord bus station, at the sea terminal on Moll de Sant Bertran and at El Prat airport. Or try Locker Barcelona (Carrer Estruc, 36; www.lockerbarcelona.com) in the city centre just off Plaça de Catalunya.

LOST PROPERTY

There is a lost property office at Plaça de Carles Pi i Sunyer, 8, close to Plaça de Catalunya; tel: 93 402 70 00 or 010 from Barcelona; Mon–Fri 9am–2pm. There is also a lost property office at the airport (T1, floor 0) open daily 8am–10pm.

M

MAPS

These are freely distributed by the tourist offices, and often left out for visitors in hotel rooms. There are also useful local wall maps at all metro stations.

MEDIA

Newspapers: A large number of European newspapers and the Paris-based *International Herald Tribune* are sold on the day of publication at newsstands on La Rambla and the Passeig de Gràcia, as well as in Fnac on Plaça de Catalunya.

Metropolitan (www.barcelona-metropolitan.com), Barcelona's monthly magazine in English, is free and has useful listings. For Spanish speakers, the handy *Guía del Ocio* lists bars, restaurants, and cinema, theatre and concert performances.

Television: The principal Spanish channels are TVE1 and TVE2 (state-owned), and TV3 and TV33, the autonomous Catalan channels. The local channel is BTV.

MONEY

Currency: The monetary unit of Spain is the euro (€). Notes are issued in denominations of 5, 10, 20, 50, 100, 200 and 500 euros. Coins in circulation are 1, 2, 5, 10, 20 and 50 céntimos and 1 and 2 euros.

Currency exchange: Banks and *cajas/caixes* (savings banks) are usually the best places to exchange currency, as they offer the most competitive rates with no commission. *Casas de cambio* (displaying a *cambio* sign) are convenient in that they open outside banking hours. Those advertising 'no commission' have lower exchange rates so you will in effect pay a hefty commission. Always take your passport when you go to change money.

Credit cards: These are widely recognised, though smaller businesses tend to prefer cash. Photo identification is usually requested when paying with a card.

Cash machines: These are ubiquitous. With displays in several languages, they will dispense money against your debit or credit card in just the same way that they do at home.

O

OPENING TIMES

Banks generally open Mon–Fri 8.30am–2pm, and also Sat 8.30am–1pm in winter. Museums are open Tue–Sat 10am–8pm, and Sun 10am–2.30pm. The majority close on Monday. The big department and chain stores remain open throughout the day, from 10am–9.30pm, while traditional shops close for lunch in the early afternoon. Usual hours are Mon–Sat 10am–2pm and 4–8.30pm.

P

POLICE

In Barcelona, dial 092 for municipal (city) police and 112 for the autonomous Catalan police. The main police station in the Old Town is at Nou de la Rambla 76–8.

POST

The Central Post Office (correus) is in Plaça d'Antoni López, at the bottom of Via Laietana, in the vicinity of the port area (tel: 93 486 83 02; Mon–Fri 8.30am–9.30pm, Sat 8.30am–2pm).

R

RELIGION

Roman Catholicism is the religion of Catalonia (and all of Spain) and Mass is said regularly in the churches of Barcelona. There are churches of most major faiths; the tourist information at Plaça de Catalunya has details on religious services, and those in foreign languages.

T

TELEPHONES

Spain's country code is 34. Barcelona's local area code, 93, must be dialled before all phone numbers, even for local calls. Dial 00 for an international line + the country code + phone number, omitting any initial zero.

TIME ZONES

Spanish time is the same as that in most of Western Europe – Greenwich Mean Time plus one hour. Daylight Savings Time is in effect from the last Sunday in March to the last Sunday in September; clocks go forward one hour in spring and back one hour in autumn, so Spain is generally one hour ahead of London, the same as Paris, and six hours ahead of New York.

TIPPING

There are no golden rules. If you feel the need to leave a tip, make it a token rather than an extravagant one. Some restaurants automatically add a service charge to the total, in which case nothing extra is needed. As a yardstick, in restaurants where a charge is not added, it should be around 5–10 percent and about the same in a taxi. In a bar or café, €1–€1.50 is enough, depending on the size of the bill.

TOURIST INFORMATION

The main tourist office is Turisme de Barcelona (Plaça de Catalunya, 17; tel: 93 285 38 34; www.barcelonaturisme.com; daily 8.30am–8.30pm). The Tourism Information Office in the Ajuntament (Town Hall), Plaça de Sant Jaume, is open Mon–Fri 8.30am–8.30pm, Sat 9am–7pm, Sun and public holidays 9am–2pm. There are also information offices at Sants station (daily 8am–8pm), and the airport (Terminals 1 and 2B; daily 8.30am–8.30pm), as well as several tourist information booths *(cabines)* located at strategic points throughout the city.

TRANSPORT

Arrival

By air: Barcelona's airport is linked by regularly scheduled daily non-stop flights from across Europe. Some flights from the US, Canada and New Zealand are direct; others go through Madrid. Flying time from London is about 2 hours; from New York, it takes about 8 hours.

Iberia, the Spanish national airline, covers most countries in shared arrangements with their national carriers (Iberia House, 10 Hammersmith Broadway, London W6 7AL; tel: 08706 090 500; www.iberia.com). Good low-cost charter airline deals can be found with easyJet and Ryanair.

The international airport, Barcelona El Prat (tel: 93 321 10 00), is 12km (7 miles) south of the city centre at El Prat de Llobregat and has two terminals, T1 and T2 (A,B,C). There are tourist information and hotel reservation booths in both terminals.

The city can be reached by train, bus and metro.

Metro line L9 Sud Aeroport T1-Zona Universita links airport terminals T1 and T2 with the city every seven minutes. The journey time ranges from 32 minutes to Zona Universitaria station to an hour to more central Catalunya or 70 minutes for Marina station. The Airport Ticket costs €4.50 (which includes transfers).

The national train service, Renfe, runs trains from opposite T2 every half hour, stopping at Estació de Sants, Passeig de Gràcia and Clot, and takes around 20 minutes. The fare is €4.10. The quicker Aerobús (www.aerobusbcn.com) departs every 10 minutes from both terminals for Plaça de Catalunya (Mon–Sat 6am–1am; €5.90 single, €10.20 return). The journey time is 35 minutes. There is also a public bus (no.46) linking the airport terminals with Plaça Espanya in the city centre.

Taxis charge about €30 to the city centre. Agree a fare before you start.

By sea: Barcelona has good sea links to the Balearic Islands and Genoa, Rome and Algiers. Trasmediterránea (Moll Sant Bertran 3; tel: 90 245 46 45; www. trasmediterranea.es) and Balearia (Moll Barcelona; tel: 902 160 180; www. balearia.com) operate ferries to the Balearic Islands; the journey takes approximately 8 to 9 hours.

By rail: The Spanish rail network has been greatly modernised. You can take high-speed, sleeper services to Barcelona from several European destinations.

Renfe, the Spanish national rail network (tel: 90 232 03 20 for

ESSENTIALS

international trains; www.renfe.com), honours Inter-Rail and Eurail cards (the latter sold only outside Europe), and offers substantial discounts for people aged under 26 and over 65 as well as families. There is also a Renfe Youth Card available.

By car: The AP7 motorway leads to Barcelona from France 160km (100 miles) to the north. The AP2 leads to Barcelona from Madrid, Zaragoza and Bilbao. From Valencia or the Costa del Sol, take the E-15 north. Your car should display a nationality sticker.

Within Barcelona

Barcelona has a reliable public transport system (see www.tmb.cat); getting around town is easy, rapid and inexpensive. Get an up-to-date bus and train *(Feve)* timetable from a tourist information office or metro station. An integrated system means that tickets can be used on buses, trams or trains. The Barcelona Card offers unlimited transport around the city plus free or discounted entry to some museums, shows and tours.

By bus: Routes and timetables are clearly marked, and maps are available from the tourist office. They run daily 5am–11pm (this can vary according to the route); there are infrequent night buses from 10.40pm–5am. For information on buses tel: 902 075 027.

By metro: There are eight metro lines, plus the Paral·lel–Parc de Montjuïc funicular, operated by TMB.

The metro operates Mon–Thu and Sun 5am–midnight, Fri until 2am and Sat 24 hours. A single costs €2.15.

Consider buying a Hola BCN! card for unlimited travel on the metro, bus (TMB) and greater Barcelona public transport for between two and five consecutive days (€14.50–€33.70).

Good pocket-sized maps are available at metro stations. For information on the metro, tel: 902 075 027.

By train: Regional FGC (Ferrocarrils Generalitat de Catalunya) trains supplement the metro with urban lines that travel to Barcelona's upper neighbourhoods – Gràcia, Sarrià, Pedralbes and Tibidabo – and to nearby towns such as Terrassa and Sabadell. For information on FGC tel: 900 901 515; www.fgc.cat.

By tram: There are two networks consisting of 6 lines, which mostly service the suburbs. For information on trams tel: 900 701 181.

By bicycle: Barcelona was the first city in Spain to install special traffic lights for cyclists. Cycle lanes in the centre are well marked, and the traffic-free port, marinas and beach front are also great for cycling. Bikes can be rented at several outlets, such as Budget Bikes (Plaça de la Llana 3; tel: 93 304 18 85) and Biciclot (Passeig Marítim de la Barceloneta, 33; tel: 93 3077475; www.biciclot.coop).

Note that the red-and-white bicycles parked at strategic points all over town are unfortunately not for rent. These 'Bicing' bikes are exclusively for resident/long-term use.

By taxi: Black and yellow taxis are everywhere and not too expensive. During the day, they are not your best option, as traffic is heavy. At night, especially if you have dined in the Old

Town, taxis are the best way to return to your hotel or continue on with the night. Hail a cab in the street or pick one up where they are lined up (usually outside hotels). A green light and/or a *libre* (vacant) sign shows when the cab is empty.

Reputable taxi companies include Radiotaxi 033 (tel: 93 303 30 33), Taxi Amic (tel: 93 420 80 88) and Taxi Ecològic 932 783 000 (http://taxieco logic.com). Check the fare before you get in and refuse a cab if the driver claims the meter is not working. Note that Taxi Amic is particularly geared up to disabled travellers as they have adapted vehicles.

Driving

Car hire (rental): Unless you plan to travel a good deal throughout Catalonia, there is no need to hire a car. Major international companies and Spanish companies have offices in the airport and in the city centre.

Drivers must be able, at any time, to produce a passport, a valid driver's licence, registration papers and Green Card international insurance, which comes with a Bail Bond from your insurance company if you are driving your own car.

Rules and regulations: Front and rear seat belts are compulsory. Most fines for traffic offences are payable on the spot. Driving rules are the same as those throughout continental Europe: drive on the right, overtake on the left, give right of way to vehicles coming from the right (unless your road is marked as having priority). Do not drink and drive. The permit-

ted blood-alcohol level is low and penalties stiff.

Speed limits: These are: 120kph (75 mph) on motorways, 100kph (62 mph) on dual carriageways, 90kph (56mph) on main roads, and 50kph (30 mph), or as marked, in urban areas.

Emergencies: In the case of a breakdown or other emergency, tel: 112. On motorways there are SOS boxes.

Parking: Finding a place to park can be extremely difficult. Look for 'blue zones' (denoted by a blue 'P'), which are metered areas; or underground parking garages (also marked with a big blue and white 'P'). Green zones are reserved for residents with permits.

V

VISAS AND PASSPORTS

Visas are needed by non-EU nationals unless their country has a reciprocal agreement with Spain. Full information on passport and visa regulations is available from the Spanish Embassy.

W

WEBSITES

Barcelona Ajuntament (City Hall): www.barcelona.cat
Barcelona on the web: www.we barcelona.net
Barcelona Tourist Information: www.barcelonaturisme.com
Spain on the web: www.tourspain. co.uk
National Tourist Office: www.spain. info
Transport information: www.tmb.cat

INDEX

Experience Barcelona
Editor: Carine Tracanelli
Author: Tamara Thiessen
Update Production: Apa Digital
Head of Production: Rebeka Davies
Picture Editor: Tom Smyth
Cartography: Carte
Photography: Adrià Goula Sarda 121; Alamy 16, 28, 32/33, 35, 48, 56/57, 66, 68/69, 75, 82, 85, 90, 104, 120, 141, 142, 145, 147, 154/155, 158; Andrea Paesante 46; AROSA Pedro Ariza/Edu Rosa 84; AWL Images 1, 4/5, 19B, 24, 29, 42, 59, 72/73, 110; Barbara Boensch/imageBROKER/REX/Shutterstock 70; Boyko Blagoev 92; Christian Romero 99; Corrie Wingate/Apa Publications 11, 30, 39, 40, 47, 54, 60, 67, 71, 81, 86/87, 102/103, 159; Daniel García Peris 160; Getty Images 6, 14, 15, 94, 100, 105, 107, 108, 109, 119, 122/123, 124, 129, 130, 132, 136, 137, 140, 148, 152, 156; Greg Gladman/Apa Publications 17T, 37, 51, 58, 65; Gregory Wrona/Apa Publications 34; iStock 17B, 18, 19T, 76, 125, 143, 144, 153; Lydia Delgado 139; Mandarin Oriental 117; Marc Goodwin/REX/Shutterstock 163; Marriott 98; Miquel Benitez/REX/Shutterstock 52; Opera Samfaina 12, 53; Palau Robert 128; Public domain 162; Ronald Stallard/Museu Picasso 74; Shutterstock 8, 9, 21, 36, 41, 55, 80, 88, 101, 138, 157; Starwood Hotels & Resorts 13; SuperStock 10, 31, 49, 83, 89, 93, 106, 114, 116, 161; Tragaluz 126/127; Vitelone 146
Cover: Shutterstock

Distribution
UK, Ireland and Europe
Apa Publications (UK) Ltd
sales@insightguides.com
United States and Canada
Ingram Publisher Services
ips@ingramcontent.com
Australia and New Zealand
Woodslane
info@woodslane.com.au

Southeast Asia
Apa Publications (SN) Pte
singaporeoffice@insightguides.com
Hong Kong, Taiwan and China
Apa Publications (HK) Ltd
hongkongoffice@insightguides.com
Worldwide
Apa Publications (UK) Ltd
sales@insightguides.com

Special Sales, Content Licensing and CoPublishing
Insight Guides can be purchased in bulk quantities at discounted prices. We can create special editions, personalised jackets and corporate imprints tailored to your needs.
sales@insightguides.com
www.insightguides.biz

First Edition 2017

Contact us
Every effort has been made to provide accurate information in this publication, but changes are inevitable. The publisher cannot be responsible for any resulting loss, inconvenience or injury. We would appreciate it if readers would call our attention to any errors or outdated information. We also welcome your suggestions; please contact us at: hello@insightguides.com
www.insightguides.com

Horaris Horarios *Timetable*

L1 L2 L3 L4 L5 L9 L10 L11

Feiners (de dilluns a dijous), dimenges i festius	de 5.00h a 24.00h	**Feiners (de dilluns a dijous)** Laborables (de lunes a jueves) Working days (from Monday to Friday)	de/from 7.30h a/to 22.00h	**Primavera/Estiu** Primavera/Verano Spring/Summer

Laborables (de lunes a jueves), domingos y festivos
Working days (from Monday to Thursday), Sundays and public holidays

Funicular de Montjuïc

		Primavera/Estiu Primavera/Verano Spring/Summer	**Tardor/Hivern** Otoño/Invierno Autumn/Winter
Feiners (de dilluns a dijous) Laborables (de lunes a jueves) Working days (from Monday to Friday)		de/from 7.30h a/to 22.00h	de/from 7.30h a/to 20.00h
Dissabtes, diumenges i festius Sábados, domingos y festivos Saturdays, Sundays and public holidays		de/from 9.00h a/to 22.00h	de/from 9.00h a/to 20.00h
Feqüència de pas / Frecuencia de paso / Frequency		10 min.	

Divendres / Viernes / Fridays   de 5.00h a 2.00h

Dissabtes / Sábados / Saturdays   de 5.00h a 5.00h